TEACHING SECONDARY ENGLISH

General Editor: Peter King

USING COMPUTERS IN ENGLISH

Also in this series

MARKING AND ASSESSMENT IN ENGLISH

Pauline Chater

ENCOUNTERS WITH BOOKS
Teaching Fiction 11–16

David Jackson

ENCOURAGING TALK

Lewis Knowles

ENCOURAGING WRITING

Robert Protherough

TEACHING THE BASIC SKILLS
Spelling, Punctuation and Grammar in Secondary English

Don Smedley

POETRY EXPERIENCE
Teaching and Writing Poetry in Secondary schools

Stephen Tunnicliffe

USING COMPUTERS
IN ENGLISH
A practical guide

PHIL MOORE

London   METHUEN   *New York*

First published in 1986 by
Methuen & Co. Ltd
11 New Fetter Lane, London EC4P 4EE

Published in the USA by
Methuen & Co.
in association with Methuen, Inc.
29 West 35th Street, New York,
NY 10001

Photoset by Rowland Phototypesetting Ltd
Bury St Edmunds, Suffolk
Printed in Great Britain by
Richard Clay, The Chaucer Press,
Bungay, Suffolk

British Library
Cataloguing in Publication Data

Moore, Phil
Using computers in English: a practical
guide.
– (Teaching secondary English)
1. English language – Study and teaching
(Secondary)   2. English language –
Computer-assisted instruction
I. Title   II. Series
420'.7'8   LB1631

ISBN 0 416 36180 3
     0 416 36190 0 Pbk

Library of Congress
Cataloging in Publication Data

Moore, Phil.
Using computers in English.
(Teaching secondary English)
Bibliography: p.
Includes index.
1. Language arts (Secondary) –
Great Britain – Computer-assisted
instruction.   2. Language arts
(Secondary) – Great Britain – Computer
programs – Purchasing.
I. Title.   II. Series
LB1631.M58   1986   428'.007'8
85-26010

ISBN 0 416 36180 3
     0 416 36190 0 (pbk.)

FOR OLIVER

CONTENTS

General Editor's preface p. x
Author's preface p. xiii
Acknowledgements p. xvi

**PART ONE:
THE COMPUTER'S PLACE
IN THE LANGUAGE ARTS**

1 COMPUTERS: IMPLICATIONS AND CONCERNS
p. 3
Computers and the Language Arts p. 6;
'Educational' programs p. 8; Computers and
control p. 11; New demands p. 15; New skills
p. 17

2 WRITING *p. 20*
'Videotext' p. 21; Word processing p. 25;
Collaborative writing p. 34; Aids to writing p. 36

3 READING *p.* 40
Screen reading p. 44; The process of reading p. 46;
Interactive fiction p. 50; The act of reading p. 55

4 TALKING *p.* 59
The management of classroom talk p. 64; Speech
synthesis and recognition p. 66; Simulations p. 68;
Using the computer to promote talk p. 70

5 RESEARCHING *p.* 75
Databases p. 78; Class activities with databases
p. 85

PART TWO:
THE PRACTICAL ASPECTS

6 CLASSROOM MANAGEMENT *p.* 95
Which computer? p. 96; Where will it be kept?
p. 103; Initial staff training p. 106; Power in the
classroom p. 110; Lesson preparation p. 119;
Organization of pupils p. 127; Evaluation p. 130

7 THEORY INTO PRACTICE *p.* 134
Case study 1 p. 134; Case study 2 p. 143

8 FUTURE PERFECT? *p.* 154
First steps – towards a departmental policy p. 154;
Towards a school policy for computers p. 160;
Towards the future p. 162

PART THREE:
REFERENCE SECTION

I   BOOKS AND ARTICLES REFERRED TO IN THE TEXT *p.* 173

II   SUGGESTIONS FOR FURTHER READING *p.* 175

III   COMPUTER SOFTWARE AND HARDWARE *p.* 177

IV   USEFUL ADDRESSES *p.* 181

GENERAL INDEX *p.* 185

NAME INDEX *p.* 188

PROGRAM INDEX *p.* 189

GENERAL EDITOR'S PREFACE

English remains a core subject in the secondary school curriculum as the confident words of a recent HMI document reveal:

> English is of vital importance in the development of pupils as individuals and as members of society: our language is our principal means of making sense of our experience and communication with others. The teaching of English is concerned with the essential skills of speech, reading and writing, and with literature. Schools will doubtless continue to give them high priority.
>
> (*The School Curriculum*, DES, 1981)

Such confidence belies the fact that there has been, and continues to be, much debate among practitioners as to exactly what constitutes English. If the desired consensus remains rather far off at least the interested teacher now has a large and useful literature on which he or she can profitably reflect in the attempt to answer the question 'What is English?' There have been notable books designed to re-orientate teachers' thinking about the subject ranging from those absorbed by the necessary theoretical analysis, like John Dixon's *Growth Through English* (Oxford, rev. edn 1975), to those working outwards from new research into classroom language, like *From Communication to Curriculum*, by Douglas Barnes (Penguin, 1976); but there are not so many books intended to help teachers get a purchase on their day-to-day activities (a fine exception is *The English Department Handbook* recently published by the ILEA English Centre). To gain such a purchase requires confidence built not from making 'everything new' so much as learning to combine the best from the older traditions with some of those newer ideas. And preferably these ideas have to be seen to have emerged from effective classroom teaching. The English teacher's aims have to be continually reworked in the light of new experience, and the assurance necessary to manage this is bred out of the convictions of other experienced practitioners. This is of particular importance to the new and inexperienced teacher. It is to such teachers and student teachers that this series is primarily directed.

The books in this series are intended to give practical guidance in the various areas of the English curriculum. Each area is treated in a separate volume in order to gain the necessary space in which to discuss it at some length. The aim of the series is twofold: to describe good practice by exploring the approaches and activities reflected in the daily work of an English teacher in the comprehensive school; and to give a practical lead to teachers who wish to try out for themselves a wider repertoire of teaching skills and ways of organizing syllabuses and lessons. Taken as a whole, the series does not press upon the reader a ready-made philosophy, but attempts to provide a map of the English teaching landscape in which the separate volumes highlight an individual feature of that terrain, representing its particular characteristics while reminding us of the continuity between these differing elements in the overall topography.

The series addresses itself to the 11–16 age range with an additional volume on sixth-form work, and assumes a mixed ability grouping, at least in the first two years of schooling. Each volume begins with a discussion of the problems and rationale of its chosen aspect of English and goes on to describe practical ways in which the teachers can organize their syllabus and lessons to achieve their intended goals, and ends with a brief guide to books, resources, etc. The individual volumes are written by experienced teachers with a particular interest in their chosen area and the ideas they express have been proved by them or their colleagues in their own classrooms.

It is at the level of the practical that any synthesis of the various approaches to English can be gained, and to accomplish this every teacher must be in possession of a rationale and an awareness of good methods wherever and however they have been achieved. By reading the books in this series it is to be hoped that teachers will be encouraged to try out for themselves ideas found effective by their colleagues so gaining the confidence to make their own informed choice and planning in their own classrooms.

Peter King
July 1983

AUTHOR'S PREFACE

We catch glimpses of truth
by means of imagination.
(Warnock, *Imagination*)

Many teachers of the Language Arts feel that the computer has very little to offer them, when, very often, the strange machine has been kept in the science or maths department or is the province of the 'computer freak' in the school. This is exacerbated if their only experience with computer-related technology is playing the plethora of computer games now available. The computer itself is seen by many people as a threat, not only in terms of jobs, but also in terms of its power to replace the traditional skills which, as teachers of English, we are pledged to promote. Yet there is little doubt in my mind that teachers who do not use the computer in their teaching are not only doing a disservice to their pupils, but are also rejecting a teaching tool which is limited in its use only by the imagination of the teacher.

The transformation of our society into a computer-dominated one is already under way: it is often argued that a proportion of the present high rate of unemployment is due to the replacement of labour-intensive industry with computer-controlled, and therefore less humanized, forms of production.

This has many repercussions for our pupils, not least of which is the sometimes enforced leisure time they will have to fill, we hope, with meaningful and fulfilling activities.

As teachers of the Language Arts, we have a unique role to fulfil in equipping our charges with the skills necessary to fill their leisure time with activities which will lead to growth rather than stagnation and sterility. I am, of course, referring to that critical awareness which we try to foster not only in our charges' approach to literature, but also to their surroundings. Until the examination years, few of us will have really constricting syllabuses to follow as our whole concern is with non-linear learning, rather than with the progressive skills of, say, mathematics or modern languages. Even if there is an agreed departmental policy on subject matter, there are not many teachers of the Language Arts who would ignore the contribution of a pupil in a class discussion which leads the class to consider a topic which was not the original theme of the lesson: the difference between a Language Arts teacher and those of other disciplines is that the former would welcome this departure as another avenue to explore, rather than dismiss it as a digression.

I use the term 'the Language Arts' rather than 'English' because I feel it describes more accurately what is at the heart of the 'subject' labelled English on the timetable. It is far more than a study of linguistics or a study of literature – we pattern our existence through language in all its forms and, as Walsh puts it:

No matter how practical or empirical an education may be, language must serve as the agency by which the teacher is related to the taught, and each to the subject of instruction; no matter how individual an education, how independent of the fluid and intricate relations constantly forming and wavering amongst the members of a group and expressed in the modulations of speech, language must act as the fine tool of analysis, the instrument of intellectual construction,

and the medium, plastic and responsive, of emotional
expression.

(Walsh, 1959)

Using language effectively is an art and that is what we are
concerned with: a study of the language of art and the art of
language, which leads to a deeper understanding of self and
experience through the exercise of the imagination. It is about
time, I feel, that we threw off the constricting and misleading
label of 'English'.

This book is an attempt to demonstrate the ways in which
teachers of the Language Arts could exploit the computer in
their teaching and indicates some of those areas which are open
to exploitation. It will also give practical advice to teachers
who have never used, or who have only limited experience of, a
computer in their classroom. Anyone looking for lesson plans
or a magic recipe for success will be disappointed, however,
because one of the strengths of the computer as a teaching aid is
the many uses to which it can be put and it is the imagination
and skill of the teacher which will determine its success in the
classroom. No book, no matter how good, will give a teacher
those attributes.

Phil Moore
Milton Keynes
July 1985

ACKNOWLEDGEMENTS

No book of this nature is ever entirely the work of one person and this volume is no exception. Thanks are due, of course, to everyone who has helped me in any way, great or small, but I wish to thank, in particular, a number of people whose contribution has been of special help to me: Daniel Chandler, who helped to plug my imagination into the computer; Peter Hunter-Watts, who started the whole thing for me; the staff and pupils at Wing County Secondary School, who, wittingly or otherwise, gave me so much help and support; Roger Siewart, Stewart Mason and Jill Sawford, who provided much-needed criticism of early drafts, and Oxfordshire LEA, who developed the superb word processor WRITE, which made the writing so much easier. Finally, I would like to thank my wife Carolyn, for all her invaluable help during the writing of this book.

The author and publishers would like to thank Open University Educational Enterprises Ltd for permission to reproduce Figure 1.

PART ONE:
THE COMPUTER'S PLACE
IN THE LANGUAGE ARTS

1

COMPUTERS:
IMPLICATIONS AND CONCERNS

It is critical vision alone which can mitigate
the unimpeded operation of the automatic.
(McLuhan, *The Mechanical Bride*)

We cannot fail to notice that computers are all around us; they are permeating every aspect of our existence, sometimes subtly, sometimes less so. Even if we do not possess a home computer, the associated technology assists us whenever we make a telephone call, watch television, use a bank account or engage in many other everyday activities. Whereas we have seen the change taking place over the past few years, the pupils we teach will have little experience of life without computers or computer-related technology and will take for granted the new advances in the same way that many of us find nothing strange in switching on a light or watching the television. From the outset, therefore, it is worth stating that our pupils will probably need no readjustment of attitude when faced with a computer in the classroom and the sense of awe sometimes felt by older people when faced with the new technology will be absent. This contrasts strongly with the initial reaction of my colleagues when I first started using the computer in my teaching: I was greeted with astonishment that I should be using what was, as far as they were concerned at that time, a machine which had little to do with Language Arts teaching. In fact, their former attitude is not unusual, nor is it confined to teachers. When the computer was set up in my classroom, pupils in my fifth-year group, who had not then had a chance to use it, often used to say, 'What's the computer doing in here?' and, when I explained that I was using it with other classes, the incredulity was plain to see in their faces. Also, after a parents' meeting in the autumn of 1984, when I spoke briefly about the potential of the computer in the teaching of the Language Arts, a number of parents approached me to say that they had never imagined that a computer could be useful in 'English'. Teachers are, of course, a conservative bunch, and a healthy cynicism is good protection against hasty and ill-considered innovation, but, when speaking to some teachers, I get the impression that their attitude towards computers goes beyond normal suspicion. It seems almost as if, in order to convince them that the computer does have potential in their classroom, I must prove that it is not only perfect in every way, but that it is far better than any other existing teaching aid. It would be, in a sense, far more challenging to ask them why the existing methods are so much better than those which become possible when using a computer: in order to answer the question, they must not only analyse what they are doing and why, but must also become familiar with the potential of the computer.

The reason for this attitude is founded mainly in the fact that, for many adults, and quite a few children, the computer is nothing but a glorified games machine. Those who own a home computer will probably spend most of their free time either playing or writing games and the number of those owning home computers is growing steadily. A survey in 1984 (see page 84) in my school, a small, rural secondary modern, showed that approximately 27 per cent of all pupils had access to a home computer and that each pupil spent, on average, seven hours a week using it – in some cases, pupils admitted to spending over twenty hours a week on their computers. The majority of them spent this time playing games, although there were some who said that they were learning to program and write their own games.

In addition to the time spent playing on the computer, most of the pupils admitted to spending a similar amount of time watching television, but this activity was more widespread with virtually all pupils spending at least five hours a week watching 'the box'. Although this survey can hardly be called representative across the country, it does paint a picture which, if repeated elsewhere (as I suspect it is), shows a large percentage of pupils spending more time on these activities than on, for example, the homework we set them. It is a depressing thought that these pupils will, in all likelihood, spend many hours every week in passive pursuits which demand little in the way of intellectual activity.

The scale of this aspect of computer use is, perhaps, more easily grasped when one realizes that Atari's earnings from home sales of the computer game PacMan in 1982 exceeded the gross earnings of the film *Star Wars*, a sum in excess of $200,000,000 (Hammond, 1984). This does not cover the sums earned in arcade games (which are unavailable for the home market), including the latest type of game, which uses an interactive video disc and computer combined to produce games with film of actual locations and 'spacecraft', controlled by the player, superimposed on it.

Play is, of course, an important element in children's learning and it would be wrong to condemn computer games out of hand. Nevertheless, those teachers who claim that use of these games aids hand–eye co-ordination, gives a sense of achievement or aids keyboard skills risk a very wasteful use of resources akin to claiming that books are useful only for the skills of page-turning. Chandler points out that these games are often used by teachers as a reward for 'good' behaviour or as a way of keeping pupils busy. He continues:

Computers are far more than video-game machines, and it is a betrayal of children for teachers to use them in a way which involves little more thought than pressing a door-bell.

(Chandler, 1984, 12)

Clearly, for many children computer games provide the reason for their initial interest in computers: it is up to teachers to harness this interest for their own purposes.

Computers and the Language Arts

The uses to which the computer can be put in the teaching of the Language Arts revolve around the idea of communication. The use of a computer involves communication between the user and the machine, either by reading or by writing, despite the fact that the computer is incapable of independent thought or action and could, therefore, be described as incapable of communication in its own right. In order to do anything, the computer must be programmed; in the same way that a book is a means of communication between the author and the reader so the computer is a means of communication between the programmer and the user. There is development work now in progress to produce what is called 'artificial intelligence' – a system which appears capable of emulating human thought processes – and, no doubt, we shall see the fruition of this work in future years. In the meantime, programmers working in the field of the Language Arts are concentrating on those areas readily accessible for computer use.

These areas are dealt with in detail in later chapters, but it is worth noting briefly at this point how the computer is currently being used in the Language Arts.

i) *Word processing*

A word processor is a program, or dedicated computer (i.e. one specifically designed for the purpose), which enables text to be manipulated on the computer screen in a variety of ways. This text, once written and laid out as the author wishes, can then be printed out — what is known as a 'hard copy'. Most word processors have various facilities to help the writer, such as a counter for words used, a facility for finding particular words or groups of words and changing them, and different means of deleting or inserting text. Some word processors have dictionaries and a thesaurus to help with spelling or repeated use of words or phrases.

Clearly, these programs can have enormous value for children who are reluctant to commit themselves to paper because of the mechanical skills involved. No longer does the lack of these skills inhibit them from writing — after all, their writing will look exactly the same as everyone else's and their work will be judged purely on its content rather than presentation. In the same way, drafting and redrafting become less of a chore, and less messy, as crossings out leave no mark.

ii) Simulations

Simulations are of two main types: some may involve placing the pupil, or groups of pupils, in certain situations in which she/he or they must play a role. These simulations can take many forms, such as the pupils being reporters on a newspaper, explorers or archaeologists, but all involve decision-making, model-formulation and testing and negotiation of relationships. The second type is where a particular model may be examined without the need for role-play, for example, a model of population growth where pupils can see graphically how various factors affect births, deaths and so on.

iii) Databases

A database is a collection of information stored on a computer. Database programs will allow pupils to set up files of information and then interrogate the data in a number of ways. This provides a means for pupils to develop research strategies and introduces them to approaches to problem-solving through manipulation of data to test hypotheses.

iv) Language development

Through various types of complex cloze procedures and text manipulation, such as code-breaking and anagrams, the computer can be utilized to focus pupils' attention on different aspects of linguistics and language use. This is aided by the computer's ability to be programmed to accept either a wide range of responses or a specific formula, meaning that the program can be designed to force the pupils to explore and extend their vocabularies in order to make the computer perform as they wish it to.

It is obvious that most of these activities can be performed in the classroom without the aid of a computer. All too often, however, these activities are bogged down by management problems and organizational concerns intrude upon the real purpose of the exercise. The computer can liberate both teacher and pupils from this handicap, as well as creating new possibilities for involving pupils directly in new concepts and new ways of thinking. I am not saying that the computer is a *replacement* for traditional English teaching – merely that it is a powerful and flexible tool which teachers of the Language Arts will find invaluable. Papert states:

> I believe that certain uses of very powerful computational technology and computational ideas can provide children with new possibilities for learning, thinking, and growing emotionally as well as cognitively.

> (Papert, 1980, 17)

Although Papert describes himself as an 'educational utopian', I feel that his claims are realistic and applicable to the Language Arts.

'Educational' programs

If we are to use the computer, we are dependent on the educational programs available and until recently there have been few programs of any real value. The software publishers have not been slow to move into the educational computing side of the business. Children who persuade their parents to buy a home computer, or who buy one themselves, form a large part of the computer-owning community. Their parents are very susceptible to marketing which stresses the educational potential of the computer and may well feel that the computer is far more worthwhile than the now old-fashioned skateboard or Rubik's Cube. A number of publishers, therefore, have brought out 'educational software' which has often had little to do with education.

Initially, the emphasis was on such 'drill and practice' programs as 'PuncMan', which, by its very title, shows how the publishers sought to merge the idea of games and education, which is not necessarily a bad thing. These programs, however, show a very mechanistic approach which has little to do with those aspects of language which Language Arts teachers are attempting to foster, nor with the potential of the computer.

One major reason for this has to do with the complete divorcing, in the past, of the professional programmers/writers from those actually concerned with education. This is hardly surprising, though, when one considers the commercial implications of computers in education for the publishers. For one large publisher, with several excellent and widely used programs, educational software comprises only 2 per cent of their turnover; yet the development costs of a good computer program are high. Robert Royce, General Manager of CLASS, a new educational-software publisher, has stated that annual sales in schools of 200 copies of a program would be considered good, but many popular programs sell 100 times that number in the shops. In fact, in 1983, schools spent about 1 per cent of their capitation on educational software – hardly a large investment, and, one would think, not enough to be an incentive for the publishers.

Royce goes on to ask a number of very pertinent questions:

To some extent the educational-software and book publishers face the same problems. Should they try to produce materials which only appeal to the middle-of-the-road teacher? Should they produce only materials which cover the main syllabuses? Or materials which help with basic skills at primary level or with exam-preparation at the secondary level? Is it the job of an educational publisher to lead or to follow the teacher?

(Royce, 1984)

These questions have, in the past, been avoided by publishers in the field of the Language Arts.

All of these considerations mitigate against the major publishers remaining in the field of educational software, except in the case of the programs they are able to sell to parents, whose evaluative skills regarding educational programs are affected more by the popular view of education, than by a deep understanding of educational needs. Interestingly, ACORNSOFT, the publishing arm of the makers of the BBC B computer, have released a number of programs designed to 'bridge the gap' between the home and the school. These programs have been designed by people who are intimately concerned with education and, thus, they have far more value than programs such as PuncMan for both pupils and teachers.

How many publishers are willing to invest in education in this way for the relatively paltry rewards remains to be seen: ACORNSOFT obviously have far more motivation than most. Their computers are backed not only by the BBC and their computer television programmes, but also by many schools (in a recent survey – Educational Computing, June 1984 – it was estimated that about 75 per cent of all schools with a computer had at least one BBC B computer). What happens when the publishers do pull out is a matter for speculation. A number of local authorities are starting to put together professional programmers and teachers to design not only educational software, but also materials to support it. Buckinghamshire, for example, are presently working on a number of modules which cross the subject disciplines and utilize the computer in varying ways. One can only hope that the resources produced in this way have a liberating effect, rather than, as some fear, providing one more nail in the coffin of contracting educational software.

The approach to the content of programs is also changing. In the past, there have been a number of programs published which form discrete units; even though they may form a term's work, they cannot be used in conjunction with other programs. They have also tended to be subject-specific in the sense that they deal with only one idea or with one skill. The new trend is to develop suites of programs able to be used in conjunction with others. For example, CLASS have published a suite of programs called CLASS WRITER and CLASS READERS which enable text to be entered into the computer and then manipulated in various ways as well as being compatible with a word processor.

Over the past two years, there has been a definite movement towards involving teachers in the design and evaluation phases of software development and this must continue if we are to protect education from the worst excesses of some of the software which has appeared earlier. Of course, for this trend to be continued, teachers must become involved in using computers in their teaching for as wide a range of purposes as possible.

Computers and control

We have already seen the commercial imperatives which have contributed to a low standard of educational software in general, but these same imperatives have another implication for education. In some ways, publishers have already started to 'invade' education with their quasi-educational programs, but this could be just the tip of the iceberg. Parents have already started a movement away from institutionalized education and there has been some wide media coverage of one or two children who have 'succeeded' with home education. In addition, large sums of money are now being invested in schools from sources, such as the Manpower Services Commission, which are outside the aegis of the DES. If schools fail to adapt to the changes which will be brought about by computers, parents will be keen to find an alternative to formal education and, no doubt, will be offered one by companies quick to see an opportunity for a new market. IBM recently produced a poster with the caption 'Will your children's children go to school?' – it is not beyond the bounds of possibility that they are being unduly pessimistic in their time scale. We must be alive to the fact that education, since 1944 in the hands of the DES, local authorities and teachers themselves, is widening its power base and, as others' voices are becoming louder, our collective voice is appearing to become weaker.

The question of control has, however, a more immediate concern for teachers: if you have watched children playing computer games, you will reach the inevitable conclusion that it is the computer which is in control of the situation. In games of the arcade type, where the user is characterized as 'Emulator' by Chandler (1984) (see Figure 1), the player is competing against the computer and the odds against him are great – otherwise few coins would drop through the slot. In some computer magazines, hints are published to help players 'outwit' the computer and build astronomical scores; there is even a book which contains strategies for 'winning' at PacMan. If we consider education to be a liberating force, then allowing the computer to control the pupil would seem to be inappropriate, to say the least. Chandler warns:

> Children are particularly vulnerable to manipulation by increasingly powerful media. If they are to survive in the 'Information Society' which has been ushered in by the dramatic developments in microelectronics, they need to be able to rely on a range of methods of self-defence.
>
> (Chandler, 1984, 87)

He asserts that there is great need for both pupils and teachers to 'develop flexible strategies for learning', something

THE LOCUS OF CONTROL

Program ◄─────────────────────────────────► User

Tutorial	Games	Simulation games	Experimental simulation	Content-free tools	Programming languages
Programmed instruction Drill and practice	Computer as player or referee	Computer as game-world: e.g. Empire-style games and the ADVENTURE genre	Mathematically based models of processes such as scientific experiments	word-processors sound and graphics manipulators databases scientific instruments control technology	Logo BASIC Smalltalk
Hospital model: user as Patient	Funfair model: user as Emulator	Drama model: user as Role-player	Laboratory model: user as Tester	Resource centre model: user as Artist or Researcher	Workshop model: user as Inventor

Figure 1   The locus of control (Source: Chandler, 1984)

computers facilitate, because, as will be seen in Figure 1, the computer allows us to focus on the process of learning rather than on content, through role-playing, testing, researching and inventing.

Nevertheless, for many teachers the use of computers in the classroom is equated with losing control (see Chapter 6). With computer programs which retain control of events this idea is reinforced. Clearly, programs requiring a 'right answer' from the user before progress is made, or which determine the sequence of events regardless of the wishes of the user, limit the computer's usefulness as a real teaching tool. How many teachers would use a book with their classes which would not allow the pupils to flick backwards or forwards as necessary? Some see a possible answer in learning programming skills in order to write programs which would be far more responsive to their particular needs. There are many reasons why I feel that this is inappropriate for teachers, not the least of which is the huge investment of time necessary to master this skill. I spent several months learning to program in BASIC, the most common programming language at the time, only to find that one of my pupils, aged 15, was a far better programmer than I could hope to be.

We are also in a competitive situation. Pupils who play the latest computer games have become very sophisticated in their expectations: they are used to superior graphics and slick presentation, elements of programming that take a great deal of time and expertise. An amateur programmer would be at a great disadvantage if he or she were to give pupils 'home-made' programs which were of a quality inferior to those they used on their own computers at home. The real danger in this situation would be that the pupils would begin to perceive educational programs as inferior to their commercial rivals and, perhaps, less worthy of attention.

The most compelling argument against teachers learning to program, however, must be that a new generation of program is being developed called an 'authoring system'. Earlier versions of this enabled programmers to translate a program in BASIC (which is relatively slow and cumbersome in operation) into machine code (a quicker and more efficient computer language). Future authoring systems will allow programs to be written in plain language for translation within the computer.

Having said that, there are some strong reservations about this view, expressed by Chandler:

> 'Educational' authoring systems, for instance, frequently either tend to encourage or *will only allow* the creation of instructional sequences in a multiple-choice format. So, whilst it is surely desirable for children and adults to use [authoring systems] when they suit their purposes, if we discourage the learning of general purpose programming languages [such as BASIC] . . . we will be responsible for creating the technocratic elite which will turn the rest of us into consumers.
>
> (Chandler, 1984, 70)

Nevertheless, I feel that, as teachers, we have far more important demands on our time than learning to program a computer. Let us rather ensure that *we* are the ones in control of educational software by becoming involved in the development process and rejecting those programs which do not serve our needs.

New demands

Outside schools, industry is finding many uses for the computer and this has a number of important implications for our pupils. I have already mentioned the use of computerized billing and computer-aided design, but these, and other applications such as robotized production lines and electronic mail, will, we are told, mean fewer people in employment, especially in the traditionally labour-intensive industries such as manufacturing. Enforced leisure may seem to some of our pupils an attractive possibility, but few who are still at school realize the dreariness of an existence without some form of employment, especially when the 'Protestant work ethic' still forms such an important part of our country's outlook. Their situation will be exacerbated if their only experience of computers, which will play such an important part in employment in the future, is restricted to the massacring of aliens: hopefully not a skill which will be in great demand!

Another implication for our pupils is that skills normally associated with the world of work are being replaced, and not only the most obvious ones. An architect of my acquaintance, who has been qualified and practising for a number of years, is now having to learn new skills as his employers have purchased a computer which acts as an electronic drawing board, negating, to a certain extent, elements of his four years of professional training. In writing this book, I have not once put pen to paper: I am using a word-processor program which, when loaded into a computer, enables me to draft and redraft what I have written with far more ease than the old technology, nullifying the many years that I spent perfecting my handwriting skills, such as they are. The question must be asked: how many of our pupils, once they have left school, will ever need to write with a pen again?

If that seems an extreme question, then consider the 'Dynabook', a concept conceived in the 1960s by Alan Kay, who now works for Atari, and considered within the bounds of the technology current in 1972. The Dynabook has been described as a 'self-contained knowledge manipulator'. It is the size of an A4 sheet of paper, can store large amounts of information and can be connected, by a number of means, to other machines. Mike Sharples, formerly of the Edinburgh Artificial Intelligence Unit, gave an example of the power of such a computer in a talk at a NATE conference at Easter in 1984:

> Consider an 11-year-old child who is writing a computer story. The story — a video game combined with written text — is a joint enterprise by a group of children, some of whom he has never seen in person, and is stored on a shared computer.

One part of the Dynabook screen shows a section of the story, the other he uses to communicate with his fellow writers. They disagree on the wording for a paragraph, so each child writes a version and they all become part of the story – the reader can make the choice.

The writer's word-processor program provides writing aids, such as a spelling corrector, a grammar checker, a thesaurus and a dictionary. It can display and alter any level of text, from the shape of a letter to the logical structure of the whole story. When the children are satisfied with the text of their story, they add in the animated sequences and then publish the completed work by sending it to a public computer file.

The potential of such a computer challenges our cosy definitions of writing, reading and daily living in a way unparalleled, perhaps, in history. May I state: this is not science fiction – the technology exists already, it is only a matter of time before the Dynabook is in existence and being used in everyday life. In fact, at the same conference, Mike Sharples quoted Nigel Searle of Sinclair, who, at a talk at Edinburgh in 1983, predicted that the Dynabook would be with us in one or two years' time *and would cost about £300.*

The skills required in the future, then, will be very different to those demanded by life, and employers, in the past. This opens up the possibility of a new division in our society – those who have ability in the use of computers (and I am not just talking about programming skills) and those who do not. But what skills will be required in the future?

New skills

There has been much use of the term 'computer literacy' over the past few years, given currency by the BBC's use of the term in association with its television programmes. Unfortunately, nowhere have I seen the term adequately defined. I believe that it has to do with understanding how the computer can be used in a variety of ways for a variety of purposes, *understanding* being the key word. This has been interpreted by some as meaning that pupils should receive lectures about how computers work, their applications in industry and their role in society. This, to me, is akin to giving lectures to pupils about linguistics and discussing the contributions of Vygotsky and Chomsky to modern thinking: it just does not work, nor is it relevant to the pupils. Just as with literacy, it cannot be taught in isolation, in one series of lessons: pupils need experience of computers in all areas of school life in order to arrive at a holistic understanding of the computer over a period of time. To take computer literacy seriously, one must, I believe, monitor the pupils' exposure to the computer and develop a school policy which ensures that identifiable and achievable objectives are met. This consideration is not entirely the province of the teacher of the Language Arts, of course. There is a far more pressing need for us to understand the impact of the computer on literacy, because, as we have seen with the Dynabook, reading and writing skills will undergo a change of emphasis, with new skills being demanded not only of our pupils, but also of ourselves.

The skills themselves will be discussed in detail in later chapters, along with strategies for their development. However, let me add a note of caution at this point: the skills I am speaking of are not susceptible to assessment in objective ways. As I write, we are promised 'grade-related criteria' for the new 16+ examinations, due to start in 1988. I believe that it would be quite easy to reduce English to a skill-based subject by turning the clock back fifty years; after all, it is easy to assess the 'correctness' of the use of inverted commas or the apostrophe, but is that what we, as teachers of the Language Arts, really want our subject to be wholly concerned with? One real danger is that the computer could be used to facilitate such an approach, negating its flexibility and potential as a teaching aid.

In the remainder of this book, I shall be showing some ways

in which I feel the computer can be used to liberate the imaginations of our pupils rather than as an instrument of Skinnerian behaviourism: let us hope that we can resist the PuncMan approach to the teaching of the Language Arts.

2

WRITING

For if words are not things, they are living
powers, by which things of most
importance to mankind are activated,
combined and humanized.
(Coleridge, *Aids to Reflection*)

Ever since the time of the caveman, some form of writing has been essential for transmitting and recording information, opinions and ideas. Subject English is, of course, a latecomer to the scene, but has naturally concentrated on this aspect of communication throughout its relatively short life and, as many may consider, will continue to do so. However, it is my contention that, although writing will have a key role to play in the teaching of the Language Arts in the future, the *nature* of that writing will change dramatically. I am not here talking about the content of what is written, although that may well be affected by the method, but of the actual mechanics of writing. The major mechanical difference between traditional writing skills and the new ones is that, when using a computer, the words appear on a television screen. Dr Stephen Marcus observes:

There are indications that what appears on television screens is neither print, *per se*, nor television. Rather, it is print-on-television: a new medium with its own characteristic messages.
(Marcus, 1983)

He uses the term 'videotext' to describe this new medium to distinguish it from traditional writing and to emphasize the differences between them.

'Videotext'

In order to show how writing with a computer is different from traditional writing, let us first consider the 'pen-and-paper' approach. To begin with, the pen is an awkward implement to manipulate. Anyone who has watched children in the early stages of writing will have noted that the fine muscular control necessary for good handwriting is totally beyond them, and it is often difficult to decipher what they have written. Nevertheless, there are very few children who, at that stage, are not immensely proud of their hieroglyphics, a situation which has changed drastically by the time they reach their secondary school, when they are penalized for bad handwriting by teachers and, frequently, laughed at by their peers. Some children compound their lack of co-ordination by adopting 'bad habits', such as writing with the lines on the paper vertical in front of them.

Marking such work can be a problem, especially when one does not wish to cover a pupil's work with red ink. Marking should be considered as part of the evaluative process, both for the teacher and, as is often forgotten, for the pupil. The problem that faces many teachers is put succinctly by Martin Wright, a teacher of 7- and 8-year-olds from a social-priority area who, in a letter to me, comments:

> When you mark a three-page story and say 'You should have developed the character more in the second paragraph and that whole section would have been better here' you don't then add 'Go and write it out again'. I would love to see children having the chance to produce a 'perfect' piece of work.

How does one mark a piece of work on which the pupil

has worked hard, yet which demonstrates basic flaws of structure?

The mechanical process of writing is, for many children, so laborious that the first draft is often the last, when most English teachers spend many hours attempting to inculcate the idea of several drafts to refine content, style and mechanical accuracy. The idea of *process* in writing is an important one, and it is generally accepted that a writer spends only 1 per cent of the writing process actually writing, the rest of the time being spent in preparing ideas, plans or headings and redrafting the original. Yet it appears that many teachers will judge a piece of writing and, sometimes, the child by the neatness of what is written.

This emphasis on presentation of work is, of course, understandable from the teacher's point of view, knowing, as he or she does, that no communication can take place with examiners, or employers, unless what is written is legible. Yet in the early stages of secondary education, there is a danger that the content of the writing can be sacrificed on the altar of neatness, particularly when it is often physical maturity, the muscle co-ordination of the hands and wrist, which is lacking. The proliferation of cheap, disposable writing implements is also, to some degree, to blame. Some years ago, only fountain pens were readily available and I can remember my own English teacher railing against the ball-point pen. Nowadays, however, children write with a greater variety of pens, each with its own characteristics, and this hinders the development of handwriting skills to a certain extent.

Another problem with pen and paper is the linear nature of writing when these implements are being used. The pen progresses across the paper, leaving a trail of words which are difficult to erase. If, when writing, one misses something out, or makes a mistake, any correction or amendment to the writing is immediately apparent. If a child is writing a 'fair copy', and that mistake or omission occurs towards the end of a page, he is faced with a dilemma: should he make the alteration or start again? This is where any consideration of content is sacrificed to expedience and, in my experience, the child will more often ignore the error in order to save work. It is at this point that we should ask whether teachers' concern with presentation could be destructive rather than constructive. For, let us be honest, how many of our pupils spend much time writing once they have left school? Unless they are continuing their education, the number of times they will have to commit themselves to paper is very small. Because those occasions are few, the importance of the communication is likely to be great – for example, when they are applying for jobs. However, these types of writing activity have little real relevance for pupils of, say, 11 or 12, and it is at this age, if not before, that a pupil's aversion to writing can start.

So how is writing with a computer different? The most obvious difference is that one's manipulative skills have no bearing on presentation, only on speed, because, these days, the QWERTY keyboard is the most common method of writing with a computer and the words that appear on the monitor or television screen are presented in the same way, whoever is writing. Consider the child who is afraid to commit himself to paper because his handwriting is very poor – if he can see what he writes appearing in exactly the same form as others' writing, how much more willing is he likely to be to write? Seymour Papert's experience, I think, speaks for itself when he states that writing with a computer is:

> always neat and tidy. I have seen a child move from total rejection of writing to an intense involvement (accompanied by rapid improvement of quality) within a few weeks of beginning to write with a computer. Even more dramatic changes are seen when the child has physical handicaps that make writing by hand more than usually difficult or even impossible.

(Papert, 1980, 30)

Papert's claim may seem grand, yet it has been fascinating for me to see that it is nearly always those with the worst handwriting who are the most eager to use the computer in my classroom. There are those who will baulk at what I have said about handwriting, claiming that it gives a child's writing individuality and expresses the personality of that child. Yet computers allow the child, freed by them from the worry of handwriting, to develop a far more important individuality in writing, that of style, which, I would argue, is a far more worthwhile pursuit for the teacher of the Language Arts.

Presentation, with a computer, does in fact have a much wider meaning, revolving around Chandler's telling phrase, 'words which dance in light' (1984, 27). Words written on a computer are ephemeral, only given permanence when printed out using a printer attached to the computer. Additions and deletions do not leave a messy blot and, because of these points, those who would otherwise be reluctant to write with pen and paper are freer to wrestle with redrafting originals without the tell-tale signs. And the final copy is presented in a very acceptable form, in relation to the poor handwriting from which the pupil may suffer.

There is an indisputable difference between writing with pen and paper and writing with a computer. That this is an important difference is, perhaps, more readily apparent when one considers that most, if not all, present-day teachers have demonstrated a mastery of the traditional writing skills in qualifying to teach and have probably spent many hours writing essays when sitting examinations using the old-fashioned pen and paper. In order to pass examinations, our pupils will also spend many hours writing in the same way, and so we, as teachers of English, give them practice in that skill: it could be said that teachers have a vested interest in promoting traditional writing skills – surely not a very convincing argument in its favour from our pupils' point of view. If, through using the computer, we can interest our pupils in the *process* of writing at an early stage in the secondary school, our task will be easier when we are promoting writing for an examination and that, although it is rather a utilitarian argument, may be sufficient for many.

Word processing

Having seen some of the advantages of writing with a computer, let us look in more detail at what can actually be done in the classroom using the computer as a writing tool. The most obvious use is as a word processor, a term which has come to cover several related activities. In the commercial world, word processors are machines used solely for the purpose of writing letters and other documents. Such a machine will cost upwards of £2000 and have many utilities for the business user, for example the ability to add a standard paragraph to a letter at the touch of a key. Clearly, few schools could consider spending the amounts necessary for such packages, nor would they need all of the facilities. However, there are some interesting word processors available for schools, depending upon which computer the school possesses. In the main, the facilities presently available on these word processors are sufficient for most teachers' needs.

One such word processor has recently become available for Research Machines computers; called WRITE, it has been developed in Oxfordshire for use in schools. I used this program in writing this book and it was my first extensive experience of using a word processor. It took me about two hours to learn to use the program fully, although I was able to start writing with it immediately. As with most word processors, one types on the computer keyboard and the resulting text is displayed on the computer monitor. Having written something, one is able very simply to delete and add text at any point without leaving any crossings out. Parts of the text can be moved very easily from one place to another and the whole text saved to cassette or disc for later revision or reference. Shaping the text is also possible, so that one can ensure that it is set out exactly as one wishes before printing it out using a printer. The program displays, upon request, such things as the number of words used, the length of the page when printed and the length of each line, which can be varied as one wishes. When printed, the manuscript text is right-justified, meaning that enough spaces are inserted in each line to ensure that there is no word-splitting.

The monitor is, of course, a set size and can only contain a certain portion of the text, but 'scrolling' – moving the text past the monitor 'window' – is easily done. This is one of the drawbacks of word processors for schools, because to review the whole text and, indeed, obtain a working copy, one does need a printer, which would probably cost a school in the region of £200. This question of relative costs will be dealt with in a later chapter, but it is worth remarking here that there may well be difficulty in justifying the expense of a printer, which in itself does not have any value away from the computer, often at the expense of other resources such as computer programs or textbooks.

Another criticism often levelled at the use in schools of the computer as a word processor is that it is a wasteful use of an expensive resource when only one person can use it as such at any one time (with the possible exception of collaborative writing – see page 34). Yet one could argue that the teacher is by far and away the most valuable resource in the classroom; in terms of economics, a teacher takes four years to train and a great deal of taxpayers' money. Yet few teachers would refuse to spend time with an individual pupil on the basis that it is a wasteful use of a resource – rather, many teachers will often engineer the classroom situation to ensure that at least some of his or her time will be spent dealing with individuals and at least part of that time is very likely to be spent discussing some aspects of writing which could be aided by a word processor.

There are, basically, two modes of use for the word processor in the classroom (for a fuller discussion of these modes, see Chapter 6), although it should not be thought that the two are discrete and unable to be mixed.

i) As the central feature

In this situation the computer is seen as the most important element in classroom activity and everything that is happening revolves around the word processor. If each child is to work for any length of time on the computer, one would need as many computers as pupils – clearly impractical in most schools at the moment. There are some schools, however, which already have a computer room with enough computers for one per child and, as the relative cost of computers falls, this situation may possibly be more common in years to come. Nevertheless, there are writing situations which can be the central part of lessons which need only one computer, such as some collaborative writing situations (see page 34), so this mode of use should not be dismissed merely because it may seem, at first glance, totally impractical.

ii) As a peripheral feature

In this mode, the use of the computer is only one of a number of activities happening in the classroom at the same time, some of which may have little to do with the computer. Alternatively, the rest of the class may be engaged in one activity while one pupil, or a small number of pupils, is using the computer. Clearly, for schools where there are few computers, this may be the most appropriate mode for the use of the computer as a word processor.

With this in mind, let us now consider practical activities which are possible in the classroom.

PROSE

One of the most difficult problems in story writing for a teacher to overcome with pupils is to encourage them to make a plan, or plot line, which is meaningful and which will help them to develop a coherent story. Quite often, a pupil's plan will consist of a few words or events without any real structure or development and only rarely will this plan be referred to in the actual writing of the story. Clearly, one should not encourage the pupils to adhere to a plan regardless of any later ideas, because, as I have stated, writing is a process and revision of the plan may be necessary as ideas develop. This, in the writing process, is called 'pre-writing' and, for this stage to be successful, editing should be kept to a minimum, so that ideas can take precedence over other considerations. Stephen Marcus and his team at the California South Coast Writing Project have been conducting research into the use of word processors at this stage of writing. He states that:

> Pupils commonly reported that when they wrote under ordinary circumstances, they usually allowed their minds to wander; rarely did they keep their attention focused undeviatingly on a single train of thought for more than one or two sentences. In addition, pupils noted that their usual pattern in composing was to interrupt the flow of thought frequently to edit and amend the language, syntax, and mechanics of their developing text.
>
> (Marcus, 1983, 118)

It was this that led them to try 'invisible writing', where the pupils turned down the brightness on their monitors so that they were unable to see what they had written. This seems, at first consideration, a rather peculiar thing to do. Yet he reports that:

> For many pupils invisible writing helped them to see how premature editing interfered with their writing, and it brought into sharp relief their own personal tendencies and compulsions in this regard. In the words of one of the pupils, 'Invisible writing helped me understand that writing really begins with prewriting'.
>
> (ibid.)

He does make the important point that for some of the pupils this exercise did not work very well, but it is obviously one activity which would be impossible with the traditional pen and paper.

One other idea currently in development is to split the screen into two parts, the idea being that one could 'scroll' text in the two windows independently of each other. This means that once having written a basic draft, pupils can see their early draft on one side, while they expand their ideas in the other half. This 'new' text could then be saved on to a cassette or disc for later amendment, or printed out so that the two drafts could be compared. Whilst comparing drafts may not seem important in the context of a single piece of writing, it provides a record of the development of the ideas which lead to a story being constructed, and this can have important side-effects for the development of writing technique. Often I read stories written by my pupils which have very good elements, yet which are wasted by a poor ending, such as '. . . and then I woke up'. If I were able to see why they arrived at this point by examining their pre-writing, I could, perhaps, give them some real guidance, rather than merely imposing my will on them by stating that such-and-such a part of their story is weak. It would help me to see where faults have crept in and point out alternatives which, hopefully, the pupils had considered themselves and rejected: I would be able to point out to them the strengths and weaknesses of the approaches they had considered.

One method of reinforcing the idea of alternatives in story-writing is seen with a very creative use of a program not designed with story-writing primarily in mind. There are books already in existence which have multiple plots, in the sense that one starts reading the story on page one and is faced with a decision, the choice the reader makes deciding which page he turns to next. Thus, a story will have several 'routes' to quite different endings. I saw these books when they were first published and felt that they could be a very interesting approach to try in the classroom, but I realized very quickly that the types of story in these books automatically appealed to boys, with the emphasis heavily on space and adventure. The other problem was, of course, that if a pupil was resistant to reading in the first place, it would be difficult to encourage him or her to read any book.

I then read an interesting paper about a program called SEEK (Jan Stewart in Chandler, 1983). The program demonstrates the use of a binary tree and primarily promotes talk and the development of classification skills through a 'Twenty Questions' approach. In her paper, Jan Stewart pointed out that the program could be used for creative writing and this intrigued me. The program allows the user to type in a small amount of text which, for these purposes, should face the reader with a decision and the answer, either 'yes' or 'no', then determines the route the reader will follow. Figure 2 shows how this works, in a very simple form. The story continues

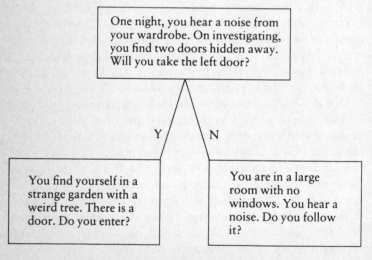

Figure 2   An example of how SEEK can be used as a branching narrative

along these lines, but users do not see the alternatives, merely the 'track' which they choose to follow.

The drawback to SEEK, used in this way, is that there is a fairly severe limit to the number of words one can use in each box, and, thus, brevity is encouraged. However, the fact that pupils can write their own stories, which appear 'magically' on the screen, hides from them (for a short time!) the fact that from one beginning, they are generating up to sixteen different endings, with the development necessary for each one.

I used this with a group of twenty-six 12-year-olds of mixed ability, although with the emphasis on the less able. Despite the fact that typing the story is rather difficult, in that one has to think 'one step ahead' all of the time, most of the pupils grasped the idea very quickly and all but a few managed to write a story. The program allows the user to print out a 'key' which details all of the decision points and where they lead. From this, I then went back to old-fashioned pen and paper and asked the pupils to make a 'book' of folded A4 paper, which used the same idea. The least able in the group managed to write 'books' which involved at least eight endings, when some of them had only previously managed to write, with great difficulty, a small number of stories. They had also begun to grasp the mechanics of story-telling, in that, in later exercises, when asked to 'finish a story' we were reading, they were able to appreciate the plethora of possibilities arising out of a crucial point.

As I have said, the program was designed for other purposes, but, had it been linked to a word processor, the story could have been extended to include detailed descriptions which would have naturally developed into a story, with each child choosing the path he or she preferred. The greatest benefit to the pupils, in my opinion, was that, whereas the published books do not give the reader real control over the plot lines, this computer program did, and all pupils could choose quite freely the elements they wished to include in the stories. In a sense, this program has been superseded by the STORYMAKER program, which is described in Chapter 4, but it did reinforce, perhaps more than that program, the multiple possibilities of plot lines. In addition, not only did the pupils thoroughly enjoy the series of lessons, but their sense of achievement in actually writing a real *book* was evident in their faces as they handed them in and the enthusiasm thus generated has spilt over into subsequent work.

POETRY

Of all the aspects of the Language Arts there are few more expressive, more which escape definition, than poetry; there are also few aspects harder to teach, especially in the later years of secondary schooling, because of resistance by pupils. Middle-school children seem to accept poetry far more readily and thus the prospect of asking the pupils to read or write it is not so daunting as it is later. I am continually faced with this problem, and I, and most teachers of the Language Arts in the secondary sector, have developed 'approaches' to poetry to interest the pupils, varying from using the words of pop songs to revealing one line of a poem at a time and asking the pupils to jot down any responses to the words. These approaches have differing degrees of success, and I am always searching for other ways to help me with my task. It would seem odd to say that a computer, which is built on logic, can aid the teacher in interesting the pupils in poetry, which is often far from logical. There are, however, a number of ways in which the computer can in fact do so.

The most startling program I have seen in this area is called ADDVERSE for the BBC B. Developed by Brent Robinson, it enables one to animate words to give poetry (and prose) a quality it has never had before. Herbert tried to give some of his poems movement by using shape, as in 'Easter Wings'; yet this is a new dimension which can, quite literally, give new life to poetry. Using fairly simple commands, a type of program is written to instruct the computer as to how the words are to be moved, written or coloured, yet no programming skills are required. This enables the programmer to emphasize various aspects of the poem as he wishes – but with the added dimension of movement: it has been called 'kinetic poetry'. An example will help to explain.

The program comes with a number of demonstration poems, one of which is by Roger McGough, author of the poem used in the BBC 'Welcome' tape. The poem is printed on the screen word by word in such a way that rhythm is achieved in the appearance of the words. In addition, the words *all over the place* appear, literally, all over the screen, emphasizing their meaning in an original and visually appealing manner. This is 'programmed' using the program and LOGO-type instructions, which do not demand what one would assume are the usual programming skills: for example, if one wanted to have the words *and fell from the sky* falling down the screen, the instruction would be: PRINT DOWN IN RED ON BLUE *and fell from the sky*. It does take some time to 'program' a poem (or piece of text), but the effort is worth it for the effects on the watchers of the text when the poem comes to life on the screen.

Another poetry program which demonstrates an interesting approach is WORDPLAY, developed by Anita Straker, which takes words and creates poems from them. The user is prompted to enter a number of nouns, adjectives, adverbs and verbs and then a structure – perhaps NOUN, ADJECTIVE, VERB, ADVERB. The program then takes words at random from each list and puts them in the pre-defined structure, creating some very interesting results. Sometimes, the output is close to gibberish, but at other times it appears that the computer has hit upon a superb combination of words – purely by accident, of course. I have demonstrated this program a number of times to teachers and it never fails to animate an audience. In one case the demonstration broke down in near-collapse because the audience were laughing so much at what the computer produced. Clearly, this is not a substitute for children writing their own poetry, but it can contribute to pupils' poetry writing in two ways: firstly, it can demonstrate graphically that words and poetry can be fun, and that is as good a way as any in which to introduce poetry to resistant learners. Secondly, it can provide the basis for pupils' work by suggesting combinations or structures of words – it encourages experimentation with words, and that is worthwhile in its own right.

Collaborative writing

In the description of the Dynabook (see pages 16–17), the example was given of a group of children writing a story together which incorporated each writer's choices of paragraphs, all of the alternatives then being presented to the reader for him to choose. Writing of this nature has the distinct advantage of being a group activity, where ideas can be advanced and rejected without the need for each child to commit himself to paper and no one pupil is responsible for the final version. In this situation, some children will lose the inhibitions they may have had sitting in front of a blank piece of paper and discussion is generated as to how the story is to develop. Added virtues are that this activity reinforces the strong link between reading and writing, and also the idea of writing for an audience, which is often a difficult concept to teach. In the past, however, this activity was probably carried out by the teacher writing on the blackboard, which is very limited by the space available and the speed at which the teacher writes – there is nothing more tedious for pupils than waiting for the teacher to finish writing on the board, especially when every pupil knows what is going to be written. Revision of the text is probably difficult, because, if what is being inserted is longer than the original, the writing can become difficult to read when squeezed into the available space. Finally, one is faced with the problem of each child obtaining a copy of the text: if one fills the blackboard and wishes to continue, one must first wait for the pupils to copy what is on the board – each at their own speed – with the consequent interruption of the main task in hand.

Purely in terms of management, a word processor is much more efficient. Corrections, additions and deletions are easier to perform; the whole story can be written without the need to 'clean the board' and copies, if a printer is attached, are easy to obtain; while the children are occupied with another activity more meaningful than merely copying. Those schools lucky enough to possess a computer room with 'networks' (a number of computers linked to a master computer) have an even greater advantage here, because each child will have a copy of the text in front of him or her immediately, which can be worked on without the need for copying. Versions of the text can, in any case, be saved to cassette or disc for further reference or revision.

Of course, it is also possible, and perhaps more worthwhile, to let a group of children use the computer to produce their own story, rather than the teacher being the mediator, with its attendant problems of choosing which suggested elements of the story should be included in the group effort. Here, the pupils themselves decide which parts are to be incorporated into the agreed version. The composition of groups becomes important – a dominant member will tend to have his or her choice included simply by force of will.

One alternative for those schools without a network is to have a rather elongated version of the game 'Consequences'. In this option, one child starts the story, writing it on the computer and saving the results. Subsequently, other children can be invited to contribute to the story, a composite version being arrived at gradually over a period of time. The whole story can then be examined and discussed, perhaps at intervals over the writing process, in order to see how the whole group feels about the results, and the pupils who started the story saying how they felt about the way that the story developed. It would be worthwhile keeping a book by the computer so that each child can note down his or her reasons for developing the story in the way they have, so that these 'jottings' can also be considered.

Another new development is linked to the 'Quinkey' – a hand-held keyboard on which are six keys, positioned in such a way that they are within easy reach of the fingertips. All of the letters of the alphabet, and the other 'function' keys, are written by pressing a combination of the six keys. This is an interesting alternative to the 'QWERTY' keyboard and pupils learn to use it very quickly. The 'Quinkey' comes with software which enables a monitor screen to be split into four parts, allowing four children to write on one screen – surely a boon for those schools with limited resources. Each child has a 'window' on the text they are writing, which can be 'scrolled', printed and saved independently of the other three. Clearly, this has implications for collaborative writing in that the four users can write the same story but when disagreeing on some parts can keep their own version.

Aids to writing

It is worth mentioning briefly work being carried out which should result in a number of programs designed to help the writer – the timescale is not clear, but it will not be long, it is hoped, before this work results in actual programs. The most important developments in this field have been reported by Mike Sharples in various sources. The work falls broadly into two categories: language work and aids to writing. In the former, there is an attempt to develop programs which will enable children to build models of generative grammars, whilst in the latter area the aim is to enable the writer to transform text in dynamic ways.

An example of the linguistic work is shown in Sharples' account of the program POEM, which has a store of story patterns on which the user can call. The program begins by building a story based on a pattern and prompts the user to type in key words at various points. As well as being incorporated in the story, the words are also stored in the program's 'memory' and if, at some future point, the child merely presses the space bar when prompted for a part of speech, the computer will choose one of its 'learnt' words at random. The child thus realizes he has entered a word as the wrong part of speech because the story becomes nonsensical. From this, the child then constructs his own story pattern, in the form: MR *name* IS A VERY *adjective* MAN, although the pattern can be as long as the child wishes. The program then generates a story based on this pattern using words at random from its 'vocabulary': the child is, in a sense, teaching the computer to write stories, but, in order to do so successfully, must appreciate the rules of grammar. (For a fuller explanation of this program and the next example, see Sharples, in Chandler, 1983.)

The text transformation program called WALTER (Word ALTERer) allows the child to see the effects of:

for example, deleting every occurrence of a selected part of speech, changing a sentence from active to passive voice, or combining sentences. A standard WALTER rule is 'relative', which combines sentences using relative clauses. The child types in, for example:

Once there was a pretty princess. The princess lived in a big castle in a forest. The forest was dark. She was very lonely because she had no friends to play with.

She then types the command 'relative' and WALTER changes the text to:

Once there was a pretty princess who lived in a big castle in a dark forest. She was very lonely because she had no friends to play with.

Clearly, programs such as these, once they become available, could be exciting additions to the teacher's armoury of tools to develop writing skills.

CONCLUSIONS

In a talk in Milton Keynes in February 1984, Anthony Adams spoke of the possibility of writing by hand in the future being a specialized skill which would not be widely possessed, and used the analogy of the monks of olden times with their illuminated manuscripts. This may seem rather far-fetched to us today, especially to teachers of the Language Arts, whose work in secondary schools is still largely seen in terms of their pupils' productive (writing) skills, by which they are ultimately judged in examinations. Yet, given the Dynabook, word processors, speech synthesis (see Chapter 4) and the already limited need for writing by hand in commerce, it is not inconceivable that this could really happen. After all, fifteen years ago it would have seemed hard to believe that mental arithmetic would become obsolete, yet our pupils are becoming less skilful at this as each year group passes through our schools, the replacement being the calculator, which is now allowed in examinations in a wide range of subjects. For this to have happened, one factor was essential – low cost. Calculator prices have fallen dramatically relative to inflation over the past few years – so much so that it is now possible to buy calculators for a few pounds, a sum well within the grasp of virtually every child. Quite where the impulse for this development originated – from the home, from the school, or from elsewhere – I leave to others to speculate about, but the fact is, it is happening.

For word processors to fall into the same category as calculators would require the machinery to be readily accessible to all – meaning at base, that the cost must be small, which it is not at the moment. Schools cannot yet afford to buy sufficient computers for all children to have unlimited access to a word processor, yet the price of computers is falling, comparatively speaking. Until they are cheap enough to be within the purchasing power of the majority of the population, writing by hand would seem to be a skill which will survive, but who knows what ten or fifteen years will bring – and children who are being born now will be at secondary school by that time. What is happening now, as evidenced in the examples given in this chapter, is that strategies are being developed to cope with the needs of the future, strategies which benefit not only our present pupils, who will become mature adults while the changes are taking place and will need to be able to adapt, but also the pupils of the future.

That is not the only consideration, however. As can be seen from this chapter, the computer is allowing the teacher to tackle traditional writing skills in new, sometimes far more effective, ways. Change for change's sake is rarely beneficial, but the computer cannot be classified in this way. It is already making a significant contribution to the teaching of writing and will continue to do so, through the development of new programs and new techniques of harnessing its power for our own ends.

3

READING

Education . . . has produced a vast
population able to read but unable to
distinguish what is worth reading.
(G. M. Trevelyan, *English Social History*)

Reading is the first of the 'three R's' and has a central position
in the Language Arts, yet its treatment in many classrooms may
lead one to the conclusion that it is not so: how many English
departments in secondary schools, for example, have a stated
policy on reading which includes a consideration of the pupils'
needs and the strategies for its promotion? It is often considered that, once a pupil can decode writing, he can read and it is
no longer a skill which needs specific attention or development,
but, rather, that it is now the level of text, and what the pupil
can produce in response to that text, which is important. As a
result, and in line with the examinations format, passages are
set for 'comprehension', designed to demonstrate a pupil's
understanding and taking the form of questions to be answered
from the text, either of the free-response type or, more recently,
as a multiple-choice exercise. It is not difficult to appreciate,
however, that the free-response exercises involve little more
than knowing how to phrase answers correctly. They usually
start with the question being rephrased to introduce a part, or
parts, of the text reproduced, by the 'more able' pupil, in their

own words: a skill which may have little to do with understanding. In some of the multiple-choice exercises, guessing can
be rewarded with a disproportionately high success rate and, in
the marking of some examinations, it is necessary to allow for
this with the application of a statistical 'guessing correction' to
the score obtained by the pupil. In an important study (Lunzer
and Gardner, 1979), Lunzer, Waite and Dolan state:

> it is a very serious mistake to suppose that the completion of
> a test and comprehension in reading are one and the same
> thing. How a student completes a test is an *index* of his
> capacity to comprehend; it is not the capacity itself and still
> less is it the comprehension itself.
>
> (Lunzer and Gardner, 1979, 66)

They conclude that it is possible to construct tests which are
useful and reliable, but that even the best ones should not be
used as the sole basis for improving comprehension skills.

In the introduction to the study, Lunzer identifies four styles
of reading: *receptive reading* – the more usual form, where the
reader 'takes in' what is being read; *reflective reading* – where
the reader pauses from time to time to think about what is
being read; *skim reading* – this is quick, to establish the subject
and to enable the reader to decide whether or not to read and
where to begin; and *scanning*, which is where the reader is
attempting to find a particular subject or point in a piece of
text. It is clear that the most demanding style of reading is
reflective reading and this is the style which most Language
Arts teachers would like to foster and which, it must be
deduced, comprehension exercises are attempting to assess. A
successful reader will, of course, switch between the styles at
will in order to comprehend what is written. The study con-
cluded that:

> individual differences in reading comprehension should be
> thought of as differences in the willingness and ability to
> reflect on what is being read. This, of course, is not a simple

characteristic. Nor is it innate. It is the outcome of many factors including reading fluency, intelligence, and interest. Also, it can be enhanced by appropriate reading strategies.

(ibid., 300)

It is this last statement which should be of most interest to teachers, for they have shown that 'reading development' is not just 'pie-in-the-sky' but a viable concept in all age ranges. Their final conclusions include the recommendation that an outline of such a programme should include:

a) the use of reading situations designed to foster a willing-ness to reflect on what is being read;

b) a structure of instruction, guidance and reading practice which improves the quality of reflection;

c) arrangements to monitor methods and materials across the curriculum in order to create the conditions under which pupils may use reading purposefully.

(ibid., 313)

It is my contention that computers can play a part in such schemes, especially in the fulfilment of the first two aspects.

It is sad, therefore, that some recent programs which some may consider are concerned with reading have very little to do with reading in the classroom. In the first place, it should be remembered that the term 'reading' is not synonymous with 'literature', a fact all too easy to overlook for teachers of the Language Arts. Secondly, just because a program is presented as concerning literature, it does not necessarily mean that it has anything to do with reading development. For example, a number of computer 'study aids' have recently been published for some of the 'classics' such as Shakespeare plays, which, it would appear, do contribute towards reflective reading. These programs are databases containing information from the plays: that is, the programs offer a means of enabling the user to search the play for various themes and character sketches. To me, they seem little more than electronic 'Cole's Notes'. It would be far more worthwhile to use a program such as QUEST and allow the pupils to develop their own database (see Chapter 5). This would allow the pupils to reach their own conclusions about themes and characters, which demands reflective reading of a text, rather than being dictated to by authors of published programs.

Chandler cites research which shows how this trend has developed in the United States:

> of 253 programs specifically for 'reading development' in thirty-two US software catalogues in 1982, fifty-six per cent dealt with word attack, thirty-seven per cent with comprehension and six per cent with 'study skills'.
>
> (Chandler, 1984, 43)

He then shows how the first two types of program, representing 93 per cent of the total, are subdivided:

WORD ATTACK

Phonics	50%
Dictionary skills	20%
Structural analysis	20%
Context analysis	5%
Sight words	4%

COMPREHENSION

Vocabulary building	72%
Literal comprehension	20%
Interpretive comprehension	8%

(ibid)

There are reasons to hope that this situation will be avoided in this country, as will be seen later in this chapter, but we should be aware that not all programs advertised as 'reading development programs' are what they claim to be.

Screen reading

How often have teachers bemoaned the fact that many pupils seem uninterested in reading what the teacher wants them to read, yet read with great intensity texts which have a more immediate interest for them, such as instructions for the construction of models, or the latest issue of their favourite magazine. This, of course, echoes the findings of the Lunzer and Gardner study. Indeed, it has been the fashion in some classrooms to use teenage magazines as the basis of work, in order to interest the pupils in reading and studying texts. Motivation is, quite obviously, an important factor in encouraging reading and computers can increase that motivation.

This has been my experience of at least one computer game. THE HOBBIT, one of the most popular computer adventure games, is sold with a copy of the book which, the instructions suggest with some force, provides important clues in mastering the game. An adventure game is a computer program which developed from the role-playing game of 'Dungeons and Dragons' and involves taking the part of an explorer, normally in a series of underground caverns, collecting treasures and solving many problems on the way. THE HOBBIT is an adventure game based on the book by J. R. R. Tolkien and the problems the player faces are taken from it. Inevitably, as situations occur during the playing of the game, the book becomes a source of important information and it is read with a stronger motivation than any ordinary classroom reading can engender. I have often been struck by the fact that, whenever I am using a computer in the classroom, at least half a dozen pupils read aloud what appears on the screen with far more interest and urgency than they do anything I write on the blackboard.

Another of the ways in which reading acquires a far more immediate purpose with a computer is demonstrated by the program ADDVERSE, although the principle is much wider. In that program, it is possible to animate text, so that reading becomes a more dynamic activity than the traditional act of left-to-right reading of text in a book. Even when writing with a word processor, one is able to manipulate text, so that it need not remain static. The effects of this on the pupils are quite remarkable: words suddenly become full of life and can create an immediate effect on what the pupil is seeing and on their progress (or otherwise) in the program they are using. In addition, the use of colour can enhance this aspect of the computer. One program which I saw in its early stages of development, GLOT by Richard Philips, allows for portions of text to be 'painted' in different colours. In the trial version of this program, a D. H. Lawrence text is presented to the reader, who can, for example, highlight the use of simile by 'painting' the words 'like' or 'as' and then review the text in order to see which occurrence of these words indicates a simile. Although this may seem to some like cracking a walnut with a sledge-hammer, for the pupils it is an exciting method of examining text and does bring the words to life – the dynamism of words is a difficult concept for children to grasp, especially given the drudgery of much of the reading they have to do in schools generally, and the computer has a unique role to play in helping them comprehend this aspect of language.

Another factor which has implications for motivation is the amount of text a pupil can see at any one time. The monitor screen is limited in size so that less text will be visible than in a book, something which can be regarded as an advantage or a disadvantage, depending upon one's viewpoint. For those pupils who are reluctant to read, the sheer size of a book, and the text within it, can be daunting – some of my low-ability fifth years refuse to look at books with more than 100 pages or so. The screenful may thus appear more appealing and manage-able than a book, in that the size of the text is 'hidden' from the user. In addition, one can concentrate upon a small portion of text in a way not otherwise possible, with no distractions from things extraneous to what is being considered. On the other hand, the screenful of text can be regarded as a handicap, because it is easy to lose the idea of the overall effect and flow of a large piece of text when it is split up into small sections. The problem is demonstrated clearly when writing with a word processor, and when the length of the text is greater than one 'screen': this is why a printer is so necessary in such a circumstance, so that one can read the whole text on paper to gain an overall impression.

The fact that there are problems in this area should in no way argue against the use of the computer, however. Rather, it should underline the fact that the computer should be used with discrimination in the classroom, for clearly defined purposes. There will be occasions, and programs, which lend themselves to the idea of a screen of text, and there will be others that do not – it is for the teacher to make the decision based upon an understanding of why the computer is to be used. For example, programs such as TELETEXT for the RML and EDFAX for the BBC, which emulate CEEFAX/ORACLE, can be used to create electronic newspapers, which demand different styles of reading from other programs, such as GLOT, where the purpose of the program is the close study of a text. Of course, no one is arguing that the computer should, at this stage, completely replace traditional teaching methods, so a balanced approach to the use of the computer is not difficult to achieve – although it could be argued that the necessity for reading long passages of printed text will diminish as time goes by and as the computer replaces traditional media.

The process of reading

In the light of the Lunzer and Gardner study, I was interested to read about an approach to the teaching of effective reading which has been developed in Australia by Morris and Stewart-Dore at Brisbane College of Advanced Education, called ERICA (Effective Reading In Content Areas). According to Stewart-Dore:

It seeks to help students to engage in and commit themselves to text. It presents reading as a continuing linguistic, cognitive and affective interaction with and response to text. . . . The focus on process strategies offers one perspective on how we might achieve literacy through reading and thus heighten students' response to it.

(Stewart-Dore, 1983)

A brief diagram of the ERICA teaching model is shown in Figure 3. Each stage consists of a number of principles from which strategies are developed, according to the purpose for which they are required. I find this an interesting way of approaching reading in the classroom because it neatly translates what I have always attempted to do into a scheme which provides, as Stewart-Dore puts it:

> an integrated language-using framework for learning. In all stages of its use, students are prompted to read, to talk about and think through ideas, to clarify, review, refine, record and justify them, orally and in writing and in various forms for different purposes.

(Stewart-Dore, 1983)

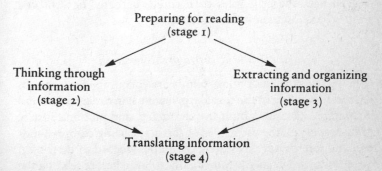

Figure 3   ERICA (Source: Stewart-Dore, 1983)

My purpose in introducing it here is to show how the computer can be used in each stage of the process, rather than to examine or explain the model in detail and, I must emphasize, this is my interpretation of ERICA. For ease of illustration, I am considering its use in terms of the class book.

i)   *Preparing for reading*

The principles involved at this stage have to do with context, ideas, text and vocabulary and give rise to activities such as role-playing from situations derived from the text and discussion of the issues raised. These activities can utilize the computer in a number of ways which go further than the more traditional approaches to them. For example, the use of EDFAX to prepare a newspaper based upon a historical period which provides the context for the book being considered for reading, or which covers 'stories' similar to the one contained in the book, can be an interesting method of arriving at an understanding of the issues involved. Alternatively, an adventure game based upon ideas similar to those in the book can be written using STORYMAKER (see Chapter 4) and the pupils, in playing the game, would then be exposed to decisions or situations with which the characters are faced in the book. In both these examples, the pupils become more personally involved with the principles than could, perhaps, be achieved with a class discussion, for instance.

ii)   *Thinking through information*

Having read the class book, pupils are encouraged to come to an understanding of the text by reviewing it in order to respond to statements made about the characters and plot and justify their responses, the principles of this stage being comprehending and interpreting. By using the pupils' record of their own progress through an adventure game, played before reading the text, pupils should be able to compare the characters' actions in the book with their own and, thus, to have a meaningful yardstick with which to measure the motivation and realism of the characters. Stewart-Dore also suggests that group cloze exercises are helpful in promoting referencing techniques, particularly when based upon key passages from the text in question. There are many programs already on the market which allow one to type in a passage for cloze work, with various features which give the procedure more impact than pen and paper exercises (see, for example, TRAY, page 52).

iii) *Extracting and organizing information*

Characterization, events and themes are the principles of this stage and there are many methods of developing the pupils' appreciation of, and responses to, these aspects of literature. The creation of a database (see Chapter 5) can help to bring an understanding of all of these elements through negotiation of its contents and structure both on a class and on a small group basis. Further, the use of a program such as SEEK to identify specific characters, for example, can create interesting discussion about their attributes and differences.

iv) *Translating information*

The work which arises from the two previous stages will help in the production of work similar, in a sense, to that done at the first stage, except that it is contextualized within the framework of the book read, utilizing information which has been gained from the book and during the three stages above. Thus, the elements are combined in written work which may be of the more traditional type, but which, as Stewart-Dore puts it, gives the pupils the opportunity to:

assume a role in relation to the text read, to explore the possibilities of a context, to choose a form of writing appropriate to a specific purpose and target audience, and to practise the craft of authoring and publishing their writing.

(Stewart-Dore, 1983)

Here, the computer can aid writing in the ways outlined in the last chapter, through the use of word processors in the drafting and redrafting of the pupils' ideas and texts.

This is an obvious attempt to foster reading in a manner which corresponds with Lunzer and Gardner's second recommendation that practice be given which improves the quality of reflection. It is comforting, therefore, that every teacher of the Language Arts will recognize in it some of the activities they have practised for many years in the classroom. This brief illustration will, I hope, show how the computer can be used in every part of the process of reading.

Interactive fiction

One of the more interesting developments in the past few years has been the appearance of books which allow the reader some choice in the stories he reads, and where the reader must make selections from a number of alternatives, the selection determining the plot followed. This can be rather cumbersome when attempted in book form, as progress is achieved by turning pages, and the flow of the narrative is thereby interrupted. Although it may seem to be 'nit-picking', when a commercially produced adventure book is being read, it is very tempting to see what is written on pages other than those the reader has been guided to by his choice, in order to see other outcomes, especially when there are attractive illustrations. When a computer is used, the reader cannot see other pages at all and he is consequently more committed by his choice. It is an attempt at what is called, in relation to computers, an 'interactive' process. This word is often misused and misunderstood, frequently being interpreted as a situation where the program user is prompted to type one-letter or one-word responses to questions. One such approach is taken by a suite of programs produced by Sussex Software in 'Critical Analysis', consisting of a series of printed passages and a computer program which asks questions about them, the user typing a letter which corresponds to the suggested answer he believes correct. It is, in effect, an electronic multiple-choice comprehension test. The limitations of this approach are quite clear: the demands placed upon the user are geared totally to the motivation the user brings with him. It can require very little thought, as an incorrect response merely brings the user back to the question with a 'hint' and he is invited to try again – a simple process of elimination, at worst, and certainly not an aid to reflective reading. In this context, there is no room for interpretation, nor for any significant dialogue, and whether any real learning takes place is a moot point. 'Interactivity' implies participation rather than key-pressing and a truly interactive program will involve the user as an important partner in the process.

I mentioned earlier (see page 44) that the adventure game evolved from the 'Dungeons and Dragons' role-playing computer game, the idea being that the player takes the part of a character and travels through a series of situations which involve decision-making in order to collect treasures. The progress of the player through the game can be seen in terms of plot, because, as the game unfolds, there are a series of 'scenes' and actions which, when put together, tell the story of the character the player has assumed. In THE HOBBIT, the character is Bilbo, and the player negotiates many of the problems which the character faces in the book. One of the most fascinating aspects of this program is that no two games are exactly alike, a problem many of the earlier adventure games had, and, just because one game is successfully completed, it does not necessarily mean that the next game will be solved in the same way or that the same situations will be presented. One's 'path' through the game is thus dependent not only upon the programming, but also upon the decisions made by the player and the random elements built into certain situations: in fact, just sitting and waiting can cause events to take place. With THE HOBBIT, the player's involvement is critical and a true interaction is achieved.

Once the user is involved in the program then, clearly, reading the information on the screen becomes very important as misinterpretation can lead to difficult situations arising. More than that, however, the game involves forming hypotheses based upon past actions and experiences. When faced with a new problem, the player must consider whether solutions to previous problems hold any clues to the present one and form some strategy for its solution. This hypothesis is then tested and its success, or failure, noted for future reference, introducing the idea of prediction as an important part of reading. I feel that this process involves a far more meaningful comprehension exercise than many presented to children in English lessons, as it demands a far wider range of skills and those skills have a more immediate and relevant purpose for the pupils.

Implicit in this type of program is the idea of multiple plot, more so if the game is different each time. The pupils can see that one decision will affect the chain of events and be aware of possible outcomes. Their involvement in the development of the plot and its dependence upon their decisions, can only increase motivation to read.

TRAY

One of the best programs centrally concerned with reading which I have seen is one available under a number of names and for a variety of computers. It is variously called TRAY, DEVELOPING TRAY, READING GLASS and CLASS READER 1, depending upon the publisher, although the original concept was the brainchild of Bob Moy. Basically it is a cloze-procedure program but it is much better than simple gap-filling, which may be a good guide to vocabulary or reading age, but which may not help to develop reading skills. When the program starts, the user is shown only the punctuation of a passage, with either a series of dashes representing letters or words, or blanks, the latter giving no idea of word length or position. The user is then prompted to complete the passage either letter by letter or word by word. In some versions, the user is prompted to 'guess', but, in the better versions, the word used is 'predict', which, of course, implies (and demands) more thought and some sort of rationale – the user must summon all his knowledge about letter frequency, letter combinations and semantics.

The thought of being presented with a screen devoid of any information but punctuation may appear, at first, a daunting prospect, but this is where the format of the program makes a difference. It is presented as a game, in which points are gained by successfully predicting letters or, for more points, words, the object being to gain a high score. It is possible to ask for help and letters are given to the user at the cost of points, which are also lost for wrong predictions. In practice, I have never seen any user ending up with a low score, because even the least able pupils have some predictive ability with the more 'obvious' words and letters. The other safeguard against pupils obtaining a disappointingly low score is that the teacher can use his own selected passage for the program, so, hopefully, the passage will be suitable for the abilities of the users.

Using TRAY in my own classroom, I have been surprised at the words which have been predicted which I had felt in advance would be beyond the limits of the pupils' vocabulary. In order to prepare one group for its use, we compiled a list of words associated with Westerns. I then wrote a short piece of text including a number of these words (to ensure that the pupils would score reasonably highly), as well as others they had not mentioned. The group took to the task of uncovering the text with gusto and soon discovered that, in the words of one of the pupils, 'That hyphenated word, three then four letters, has just *got* to be six-guns', which led to a minor discussion about hyphens. It was very noticeable that every pupil suggested a number of possibilities, even one girl who had not spoken out loud for the three months during which I had taken that class. Another spin-off came from the fact that the end-of-lesson bell interrupted our deliberations, and we had to return to the text two days later. Knowing the limited memory span of my charges, we started from scratch again: it was stunning to find that many of the pupils could recite the parts of the passage we had uncovered two days before almost word-for-word and that they had been considering some of the more difficult gaps since the previous lesson. This was in complete contrast to the normal procedure teachers have to carry out when a reading activity has been interrupted at the end of a lesson: that is prompting the class to give a résumé of what has been read previously, knowing that many will have forgotten. The whole exercise was voted a great hit by the pupils and the ensuing discussion about the passage was undertaken with enthusiasm and a much greater insight into its meaning, I'm sure, than would have been in evidence if I had presented it in the traditional way.

One problem I have found with published cloze tests is that, quite often, pupils' responses are better than the 'correct' answers. The difference between those and TRAY is, of course, that the users have no impression or ideas about the passage when they start. However, there is still a correct answer with the computer program, so why is this different in any substantial way? The answer to this lies not only in the novel presentation and the fact that a great deal more semantic work must be done in decoding the text in the first place, but also in the 'scratchpad' facility present in the better versions. This is a 'page' which can be requested by the user at any time, but which will appear unrequested at various stages during the program, for the user to type in any thoughts about the passage. When the passage is completed, this scratchpad can be printed out to provide a (to be honest, partial) record of the thought processes which went into the decoding of the passage. This can form the basis of an extremely good discussion about the process of decoding, and can often show users how particular 'cues' led to conclusions being drawn, particularly when the program lends itself to group, rather than individual, use. In the Lunzer and Gardner study, the use of group discussion activities is considered and it is possible to apply their conclusions to the use of TRAY:

> a situation has been created where immediate responses can be aired and argued out. The reader is no longer left to his own internal thoughts. The assumptions of the writer can be questioned and explanations offered, thus making more explicit the communication between writer and reader.
>
> (Lunzer and Gardner, 1979, 310)

The act of reading

Finally, it is worth remarking that all that I have written in this chapter should be seen in the light of the changed (and changing) nature of the act of reading. Lunzer and Gardner's study starts from a consideration of the differences between the two receptive modes, listening and reading, and suggests that there are seven main reasons why reading is more demanding than listening. If we examine these seven reasons in the light of the new technology, we may gain some insight into the changes brought about by computers.

Firstly, they note that, 'There is no common situation. The "situation" (or frame of reference) that is invoked is contained in the text and must be inferred from the text.' On the surface, this is unchanged with the computer, except for the important distinction that it is a new medium, and, in McLuhan's words, 'the medium is the message', so the situation is significantly different for the reader of computer text, who will probably have different expectations of a computer than those a reader will bring to a book.

Next: 'The words stand alone. They are not supported by non-verbal behaviour or by verbal expression.' Apart from the possibility of speech synthesis (see Chapter 4) to support the written word on the computer screen – an exciting possibility in itself – there is now great potential in the animation of text: the words need no longer be static, but can be made to move, to be dynamic, and the control the user can exert over text makes reading far from passive. In addition, the ability to highlight text in other ways, by colour or typeface for example, which is extant now in printed texts, can be achieved very simply in a manner not possible with the old technology.

The third distinction is that, 'There is no possibility of feedback to the source. . . . This is because the readership of the text is not known to the writer.' With the arrival of electronic mail and systems such as The Times Network for Schools, which allow for almost instantaneous written communication between users, the ability of readers to contact the source of text very quickly clearly changes this aspect of reading. While it will perhaps not be possible for individuals to contact authors of substantial texts at will, it is possible that authors will be able to provide alternative texts for particular audiences via the computer. For example, in reviewing this book in six months' time, I am sure that there will be parts I will wish to alter or expand on (the volatile nature of the information I am considering makes this inevitable), but the nature of the printed book makes this expensive and impractical: if this were distributed electronically, I would be able to update and alter this text very quickly and easily.

'Reading is uninterrupted, monotonous,' is the next distinction, by which Lunzer and Gardner mean that, 'There is little opportunity for overt response on the part of the reader . . . The writer knows nothing of it. . . . This presents a problem of motivation.' Apart from the ability of the computer to give text dynamism and thus make reading far less monotonous, the interactive nature of reading on the computer gives far more scope for author/reader interchange. With adventure games, for example, reading is reinforced and reflective reading given rewards in the form of achieving a specific goal, such as obtaining treasure or reaching the next stage of the game. The writer is, therefore, able to anticipate particular responses by the reader.

Fifthly, 'The editing of text can stand in the way of comprehension. The very errors and hesitations of spoken language correspond to the sticking points in the movement of the speaker's thought. They signal difficulties and offer time to overcome them – for the listener as well as the speaker.' In written text, these 'indicators' are absent: it would be difficult, perhaps, for a reader of this book to perceive which points caused me the greatest difficulty in explanation or phrasing (or, more importantly, the thought-processes which led to the final formulation) and the presentation of the text seems to imply that all points have equal force. Here, the idea of the 'scratch-pad' in the program TRAY (see page 54), where the 'developer' can note some of the thought-processes involved in the uncovering of the text, can aid the reader's understanding by indicating the steps which led to the final argument and arrangement of words.

The sixth point made by Lunzer and Gardner is that: 'Because text is more complete than utterance, it tends to be more dense. To the immature reader, it is also unfamiliar in choice of words and in style: the language is his own, the style foreign.' The burden on the reader is thus increased with text. But, as has been indicated in relation to other points above, computer text is so much more flexible than the printed version, and the ability of the computer to provide 'services' to the reader, such as a dictionary and thesaurus, can make consultation of other sources for elucidation of difficult words or phrases that much easier and the text that much more accessible. In addition, I have already mentioned (page 45) that the screen limits the amount of visible text, and this may well have some effect on its perceived denseness and difficulty.

Finally, 'The writer orders his material. But the order which he thought best may not be best for the given reader.' Again, the flexibility of computer text allows for the easy manipulation and ordering of material to suit the reader.

It can be seen, therefore, from this very brief consideration, that the computer can alter and is altering the very act of reading. In the light of this, it becomes even more important for teachers of the Language Arts to adapt their teaching strategies to take this into account. However, it is also worth remembering that Lunzer and Gardner do make the point that printed text is an excellent medium for learning simply because it is permanent and can be 'revisited' at will, whereas computer text can be seen as transitory. Perhaps it is time for some research into how much computers can offer to the learning process in breaking down the difficulties with which immature readers are faced: without doubt, such research would aid teachers in deciding which medium is best suited for their purposes.

CONCLUSIONS

As has been shown in this chapter, it is possible to use the computer in a variety of ways to promote reading, but developing a scheme which utilizes computers as part of an overall strategy is preferable to a piecemeal approach. In devising such a scheme, consideration should, of course, be given to the 'local conditions', such as the age, ability and interests of the pupils, and should also acknowledge the recommendations of the Lunzer and Gardner study, which have been dealt with only briefly here. Used well, the computer can provide much-needed motivation and an exciting context for reading, but if it is used in an ill-considered way, it could, equally, prove a hindrance: it is a 'two-edged sword'.

4

TALKING

He gave Man speech, and speech created
thought, which is the measure of the
universe.
(Shelley, *Prometheus Unbound*)

Since the early sixties, when Wilkinson gave us the term 'oracy', the role of talk in the classroom has grown in importance; yet one cannot help but get the impression that it is still treated as the 'poor relative' of other activities in the Language Arts classroom. Allen argues:

> When one looks now for help with understanding the relation of talk to writing or reading, one finds little convincing help. Yet in 1965 *Spoken English* already defined the problem. 'The task ahead is to define [oracy] in terms of particular skills and attainments, for different ages, groups, circumstances; to discover the best methods of teaching it; to bring it into synthesis with other work, especially that designed to promote literacy.' We are in English teaching little further on in defining it.

> (Allen, 1980, 118)

We see talk attaining some position in CSE examinations, but as a very small element in the overall grade, and guidelines for marking, where they exist at all, are vague. Further, whereas there is a vast literature in the promotion of reading or writing, there are few books offering any advice on the promotion of talk in the classroom. Even 'course books' pay only lip service to talk, by including sections headed 'Discussion Work' with assignments which merely ask pupils to discuss topics or items covered in previous sections. It seems strange that this should be the case, as the management of talk in the classroom can be very demanding on the teacher's skills and patience.

It does appear, however, that progress is being made in Scotland, where the new Standard Grade Arrangements are to be implemented in 1986 which will give 40 per cent of the total assessment to talk and listening, acknowledging that they do have an importance not reflected in other examinations in English around the country. Some cynics will say that this is no recommendation and in a sense they are right, because it appears that, whilst the proposals encourage a definition of the various skills which Allen mentions, they go no further in bringing talk into synthesis with other work.

In the document issued by the Scottish Examinations Board, an explanation of the weighting given to the various aspects of the assessment is given:

> The decision to apply an extra weighting in the aggregation to the traditionally established modes of Reading and Writing reflects the Board's awareness of the far-reaching implications of introducing assessment of Talk and Listening. It also recognises the degree of confidence which exists among teachers, and the public, with regard to Reading and Writing. When similar confidence has been established in assessment of Talk and Listening, this weighting will be reviewed.
>
> (Scottish Examinations Board, 1984)

One wonders quite whether the important consideration in this explanation is the degree of teachers' confidence or whether it is the public's. This question is raised again when it is stated that:

> The external assessment of Listening is similarly intended to

allow teachers time to gain confidence and expertise in handling a mode which is relatively unfamiliar to them.

(ibid.)

Regardless of any other implied meanings, this statement does indicate that the concept of oracy, which includes listening, is felt to be new to teachers, which is why they would find it difficult to assess. This view, if true, would reinforce Allen's assertion that teachers of English are no further forward in defining oracy, promoting it in the classroom and bringing it into synthesis with other aspects of the Language Arts.

Even cynics would have to agree that the inclusion of talking and listening in examinations in English reflects a growing awareness of their importance in the teaching of the Language Arts – a fact which will have a 'knock-on' effect for middle and primary schools. However, it is obvious from the Scottish proposals that oracy is being considered as a skills-based concept, and assessed as such. The criteria for the elements of the examination are described as 'generalizations', and there is an exhortation for teachers to undertake a 'continual process of adjustment' in order to achieve a 'holistic assessment of a pupil's performance'. Nevertheless, the use of the word 'performance' stresses the artificiality of this type of assessment. Further, although having stated that the criteria are 'vignettes rather than inventories', the Board recommends that:

> When performance in Reading or Listening is to be assessed by multiple-item comprehension tests (as in the conventional Interpretation paper), it is recommended that the GRC should be consulted in designing appropriate test items and marking instructions.

(ibid.)

Not only is the Board intent on using an unreliable measure of comprehension (see Chapter 3), but it is also compounding the unreliability by basing the measure on what are conceded as being only generalizations.

But what of the criteria themselves? The criteria for a Grade One in Talking include, under the heading of 'Intelligibility', a statement that:

> Given opportunity for preparation he [the examinee] will be readily intelligible without the need for support through prompting and questioning. Voice (i.e. audibility *and enunciation*), delivery (i.e. pace, *fluency and modulation*) and content (i.e. ideas, structure *and language*) will combine to achieve telling impact.
>
> (ibid. – *my italics*)

The implication of the words I have emphasized in the above statement is that the pupil will be judged as much by social class as by communicative ability. As Allen states:

> We should be ready to draw on the best that there is in accepting local life in language, while discouraging any expression that is ineffective, or unsuccessful, just as we would with any other kind of speech. To help children to realise the possible social disadvantages of a particular way of speaking is not the same as being a dedicated agent in the inquisitorial eradication of that way in our pupils. . . . to deny them utterance is to deny them the chance to connect the life of the classroom with the life they live outside.
>
> (Allen, 1980, 129)

The Scottish Examinations Board do state that:

> Unless the particular purpose of Talking renders it inappropriate, *features* of accent or dialect are perfectly acceptable.
>
> (Scottish Examinations Board, 1984 – *my italics*)

but this does not make it clear: are only selected aspects of accent or dialect to be accepted, or does it mean that they will be accepted only if they do not intrude upon the 'purpose of Talking', whatever that may mean?

Another aspect of this development is that it fails to recognize the exploratory nature of talk in its pattern of assessment. We use talk to explore and explain experience and ideas; yet there cannot be an objective measure which we can apply to it. The Scottish proposals, although acknowledging that talk performs this function, fail to solve the problems they raise. Looking at the criteria for a Grade One in Talking, will a pupil who, in being examined, falters in attempting to express an idea, or who struggles to use spoken language to pattern his experience, be less successful than a pupil who has learnt a speech parrot-fashion in the time given for preparation? One would hope not, of course, but I fear that it will be up to the already hard-pressed classroom teacher to make some sense of these proposals in order to ensure that the assessment is positive in emphasis rather than negative.

The Scottish proposals are to be applauded in that they have, at least, attempted to widen the scope of examinations in English and they do point out the dangers inherent in such an exercise. To attempt to reduce vital and dynamic aspects of language into constituent, *but not discrete*, elements appears to me to be foolhardy. Those elements may be assessable in some way, but can we really pretend that the results of such an assessment are in any way meaningful? Teachers may well understand the dangers, but these examinations are going to be used by the pupils in seeking employment or further education and employers and further-education establishments tend to regard examination results as predictors of future performance: when they see that a pupil has a Grade Four for Talking, what will that actually mean to them? I do not, of course, wish to argue that we should ignore oracy: there is a great need to encourage our pupils to refine their spoken abilities in various contexts for various purposes. However, the terms 'important' and 'examinable' are not synonymous and we take great risks with our pupils if we consider them so.

The management of classroom talk

It would be difficult to assess accurately how talk is managed in classrooms throughout the country, but one would hope that the situation has progressed from that described by Wilkinson:

> The conventional educational situation imposes a receptive not a productive language role on the pupil. It has given one-way communication, from the teacher to the taught.
>
> (Wilkinson, 1965)

This describes the usual course of lessons where there are no contributions of any purposeful nature from the pupils – that is, where the teacher is merely searching for a 'right' answer or a 'correct' response. Whole-group discussion (surely a contradiction in terms if ever there was one) often has the same result, with few pupils actually contributing anything. If there is going to be any meaningful discussion between members of a group, the group must be small and each member of the group must feel that their contribution will be valued by the others. Often, of course, this means that the teacher must know when to withdraw or stay silent, despite the temptations not to do so, particularly when he does not realize that his presence can have an inhibiting effect on the pupils. Classroom discussion (or talk) is, I believe, one of the most difficult of teaching skills to perfect.

Problems do arise with small-group talk in the classroom which often prevent teachers from using it as often as they might. There is still a sense in which one is judged as a teacher by the amount of noise emanating from one's classroom and several small groups all talking (and, often, shouting) at the same time creates more noise than no talk/discussion with a whole group. This is especially true in secondary schools, although perhaps less so in middle and primary schools which have practised small-group work for many years and given the pupils a good grounding in the self-discipline necessary for such work to be successful. I find that pupils in the first year of secondary schooling find it far easier to cope with small-group work than those higher up the school, perhaps because the older pupils become, the less chance they have to work in this manner. One must, of course, have a great deal of confidence in the group as a whole to allow them to split into small groups where the teacher will be, of necessity, absent for part of the time. It would be a little idealistic to imagine that each group will spend the entire time discussing the chosen topic, so there must be an element of trust in the relationship between the teacher and the pupils in this type of activity: teachers in primary and middle schools, where they will tend to spend longer periods of time with particular groups, will have more opportunity to develop that trust.

These, and other related problems, are basically concerned with management, a topic which will be discussed in Chapter 6. Nevertheless, it is worth noting here that the computer can fill the role of 'teacher's assistant' in group-talk situations. Several groups working on different tasks can stretch the teacher, but if one group is working on the computer, which is providing some degree of control over the task in hand, then the teacher can concentrate on a smaller number of groups – the task of the teacher is thus eased slightly. It has been my experience that, unless there is a problem with the computer or the program, the group working on the computer will seldom need attention from the teacher and there are few occasions when they will stray from the task set. It is important to realize, though, that the computer cannot provide a substitute for the teacher, even though it may help to ease classroom-management problems. If computers could take the place of teachers, we could merely provide each pupil with a computer and take early retirement! In practice, when I have used a computer with my pupils, I have found it a great temptation to watch the group on the computer perhaps more than other groups, because it is fascinating to see how the group interacts and reacts to it. Just as one needs to appreciate when to intervene in discussion and when to stay silent, it is important to learn to live with the computer in the classroom.

Speech synthesis and recognition

One development which could change our entire attitude to computers, not to say our teaching, is speech synthesis and speech recognition. The two are very different and a distinction needs to be drawn. Speech synthesis, already with us in a number of applications, is the ability of a computer to simulate speech. We already have a camera which tells us the correct exposure and speed settings, a car which tells us to fasten our seatbelts and, at the Motor Show of 1984, we were promised that many more warning functions in cars will be performed by speech synthesis. To program such a facility in a school microcomputer would take up a great deal of memory space, leaving little for a program to perform other functions, but the developmental work currently taking place is geared towards the production of chips with a larger memory, and it may soon be possible either to buy a computer complete with speech synthesis which does not reduce the amount of memory, or to buy chips which can be fitted into existing computers, which will give the computer a speech-synthesis capability.

Speech recognition, on the other hand, is the ability of a computer to recognize and interpret spoken commands. The Apricot computer, launched in 1984, has a limited speech-recognition facility, and in the initial advertising we were shown a businessman asking (literally) the computer to show him the latest sales figures, which it very obligingly did. The technical problems of speech recognition are obvious, because the computer needs to cope with such things as regional accents and dialects, poor enunciation and screening out 'noise' – for example, if the businessman in the Apricot advertisement had said, 'Could you please show me the most up-to-date figures for sales in the current fiscal year', would the computer have understood? In order to do so, it would need to be programmed with a large vocabulary including synonyms and grammatical structures, again using up a great deal of memory space. Nevertheless, the fact that Apricot used this as a major selling point indicates that we shall, no doubt, see computers in the future with some form of speech recognition.

The implications of these developments for all computer users are vast, but the implications for education are, perhaps, more far-reaching: imagine a situation where one need not be able to write, or spell, correctly, because any written communication can be effected by merely talking to a typewriter/ computer. I have already seen a prototype which will type a letter, correctly set out, spelt and punctuated, operated purely by voice. If this were the case, and many people believe that the situation will arise within the next ten years, would we be teaching an outmoded and inappropriate set of skills if we continued to give writing more importance than talking? It has been suggested by Anthony Adams (in a lecture in Milton Keynes in 1984) that writing will become a skill of the few, rather as manuscript illumination was practised largely by monks. In such a situation, talking will become as important for the teacher of the Language Arts as writing is today. The idea will, no doubt, fill some with horror, but do remember that writing as a common skill has been with us for a relatively short time when compared with speech.

The development work necessary for that scenario will, no doubt, take time, but not as much time as we might like to think. It is possible now to purchase a speech-synthesis unit (which takes virtually no memory from the computer) to plug into most types of home computer for as little as £25 and in the October 1984 issue of *Your Computer* there is a program-listing for a speech-recognition facility for the ZX81, now one of the more primitive home computers. It cannot be long therefore before computers will talk to us and we to computers, but whether this will call for a new mode of talk remains to be seen. As teachers of the Language Arts, we should be aware of the possibilities and dangers of speech synthesis and recognition and be prepared to cope with their consequences.

Simulations

A most interesting type of computer program for use in the classroom is simulation, which can take a number of forms. At one end of the spectrum, a simulation will demonstrate the workings of a particular machine or process which would normally be impossible in a classroom setting, because of expense, safety or other practical considerations. At the other end of the spectrum, a simulation will call on a pupil, or pupils, to role-play in a given set of circumstances. For ease of consideration, I would like to make a distinction between computer-managed and computer-based simulations. The former name I will use to indicate a situation where the computer acts as an arbiter and provider of parameters, the main action happening away from the computer. Such a program is KINGDOM, of which there are many versions. In this program, a group of pupils can act as rulers of a country, deciding how much food to grow, to store or to release to their populations. The real work in deciding the balance which must be struck between the various elements is done away from the keyboard. Having come to a decision, the group uses the computer only to see what the results of their deliberations are. I take computer-based simulations to mean programs where the main work is done on the computer, such as with a program which demonstrates a particular process or machine. One such program, available under many different names, simulates population growth according to a number of factors which can be varied by the user.

Language Arts teachers using simulations tend to use the computer-managed variety because of the explicit nature of the decision-making necessary. However, teachers should be extremely clear in their own minds as to why they are using a particular simulation: as an enjoyable way of learning content, or as a way of examining process. A particularly good example of a computer-managed simulation is SAQQARA, which places pupils in the role of archaeologists excavating the Egyptian site of that name. The program demands decision-making by the pupils which entails group discussion and co-operation, but whether or not the pupils learn more about the program's content (archaeology, Egyptian history, etc.) or about the processes of decision-making depends a great deal on the teacher and the gloss he puts on the activity. There is no doubt that programs such as this do require a great deal of pupil interaction, but many pupils would take more interest in the discovery of 'finds' than in the processes which enabled them to make that discovery. This is not to say that computer-managed situations cannot be used to help pupils to explore the decision-making process: as Chandler states, these programs

> have at least the potential to focus discussion on a shared experience without intervening and controlling the shape and language of the discussion as teachers almost invariably do.
>
> (Chandler, 1984, 24)

Whilst Chandler goes on to voice serious doubts about how meaningful these processes are in relation to real-life decision-making, there is no doubt that such programs do stimulate discussion in the exploratory mode. His later assertion that adventure-type games do not have the pitfalls of other computer-managed simulations I find difficult to accept, for, although the situations facing the players are imaginary and thus focus attention far more on problem-solving than on content, the object of the game, to find 'treasure' or escape from tricky situations, can still mask the object of the exercise – again, it is for the teacher to provide the context.

Despite this, there is little doubt that simulations do provide an excellent framework for talk in the classroom. The problems which pupils face force them to discuss possible solutions both within their groups and with others. I have found this true not just of simulations, however: virtually any work with the computer produces talk of one variety or another, if only because the medium is new to the pupils in the Language Arts classroom. This will not last, of course, as the computer becomes a familiar feature of the classroom and of their lives in general, but their enthusiasm is there to be harnessed, at least for the moment.

Using the computer to promote talk

In view of the foregoing considerations, I was very pleased to see a program being developed in Scotland, under the auspices of the SMDP, called NEWSDESK. This simulation is concerned with the preparation of items for inclusion in a radio or television news broadcast. (The program is designed for use on a computer network, where a number of computers are connected together.) Each group of pupils is asked to select a type of story to cover – sport, entertainment and so on – and is then given a choice of news items under that category, the bare facts of each story having been typed in previously by the teacher. Each group must then expand on the bare facts, resulting in a script for the newsreader, and send it to the editorial group, via the computer, for acceptance or rejection. This process is complicated somewhat in NEWSDESK by the fact that, at some stage during their writing, each group will be presented with a 'newsflash' to write, which will mean dropping one of their original stories and 'fleshing out' the bare bones of the new story in a short time.

The beauty of this program is that it leads naturally to many other topics, but is still centrally concerned with talk over a range of subjects. In the first instance, the group must decide which stories to write, then actually write them, a process which demands decision-making, negotiation of roles and collaborative writing. The stories having been written, the 'newsflash' will demand a decision about which item to drop. The new item will then have to be written and sent to the editorial group which will have to decide the items to include in the 'broadcast'. Finally, the 'broadcast' has to be made and an assessment sought from the group as a whole.

Although the program is still in development, I feel it worthwhile to quote from a letter I received from one of its development team, Richard Pugh, who has used an early version in his classroom.

> The air of urgency was electric and I was astonished to witness a group of students, usually moved to apathy by Eng. Lit., produce enough adrenalin to stun a whale. Partly, I must admit, this atmosphere was aided by a loudly-ticking stop-clock, borrowed from the Science Department, which I had placed in a prominent position. . . . While the stories were being composed it was of great interest (and caused some amusement) to note that not a few were rejected and returned to their writers to be revised or rewritten. In the final stages it was up to the news readers to decide how best to link the various items. . . . It was final proof for me that not only does the computer have a place in the teaching of English, its place *is* in the teaching of English.

It is clear that such a program could be a superb teaching aid and I look forward to its completion with great anticipation.

One of the advantages of this type of simulation is that it is content-free: that is, the subject matter is provided by the teacher and can be varied to suit the circumstances. For example, it is a fairly well-tried strategy to create a newspaper around a class reader in order to stimulate discussion and thought about the text. Using NEWSDESK adds a new dimension to this activity – a radio news broadcast about the situation surrounding David's escape in *I Am David*, for example, could provide an interesting way of stimulating discussion of the text.

Adventure-type games are also entering a new phase with the trials of a program called STORYMAKER which enables the writing of adventure games around situations defined by the user. This will be welcomed by those teachers who have had to use commercial adventure games which allow no variation of plot, because they (and their pupils) will be able to write games which start, for example, from situations encountered in class readers, thus adding another dimension to discussion. It is too early to comment on the trials, but it does seem to me that STORYMAKER has great possibilities in the classroom.

Using an adventure game in the classroom to promote talk of all kinds can present a few problems, however. One of the biggest problems, especially for the teacher in a secondary school, is the time factor. Most adventure games need a fair investment of time, and where there is only one computer in the classroom, continuity can be lost very easily. It is in this circumstance that a printer can be very useful, for the pupils can retain a printed record of their experiences, which will not only be a reminder for them in future lessons, but can also form the basis of some creative writing, representing, as it does, the 'plot' of their story. Without such a record, any discussion about events, strategies employed or decisions reached is extremely difficult. When I did not have a printer available (the game I was using did not have a printer option anyway), I asked each group to keep a log. From these logs the groups were able to 'compare notes' and discuss the differing approaches to the same problems. In addition, the filling in of these logs caused a fair amount of discussion about what had happened anyway, so perhaps this is an idea worth using even if there is a printer available, although there would then be no necessity to record exactly what had happened during play.

The word 'play' does have another meaning, of course, and this element of computer programs can be used to promote talk in the classroom, particularly when there is an element of competitiveness. In the last chapter, I mentioned the program TRAY, a cloze procedure program presented as a game in which the object is to fill in the blanks and obtain the highest score possible. I have used this program in my classroom with small groups taking it in turns to suggest words or letters, keeping a careful note of the effects of their suggestions on the score. Whilst not perfect, it is an interesting way of introducing the program to a class and, with the competitive edge, the talk within the groups becomes very purposeful. Another program geared more to use in this fashion is SLYFOX, by the ITMA Collaboration. A fox is hidden on a farm and the object of the game is to discover its whereabouts. The pupils are provided with a map of the farm, which is divided into a number of areas, and they must, by a process of deduction, identify the fox's hiding place by name. The program has a number of 'modes', including a 'Mastermind' format (the board game rather than the television version!) where the group can make a guess and the computer indicates by stars that they have some parts of their guess correct, although which parts are correct is not revealed. After playing this a number of times, the pupils develop strategies which will deliberately mislead other groups: for example, they will have decided that the fox is in one area, yet guess another area, hoping that other groups will be deceived. Of course, the strategies they develop will have little relevance outside the context of the game, but it is the forming of those strategies and the talking and listening that goes on which is important.

CONCLUSIONS

If the inclusion of talking and listening in the Scottish examinations is any indicator to what is going to happen generally, much work needs to be done. Indeed, we are promised Grade Related Criteria for the GCSE, although there is a possibility that we might escape them for the time being. However, whatever happens we are little further forward in relation to oracy than we were twenty years ago. As Allen has indicated, we are not clear about its relationship to other aspects of literacy nor the best methods for teaching it. There is, of course, little doubt that teachers of the Language Arts have been attempting to promote oracy in one way or another for many years, but it does look as if we face a future where oracy, for the first time, will form a large constituent part of examinations and we must be prepared.

Other aspects of oracy need further investigation, particularly in the light of the new opportunities arising out of the use of the computer in the classroom. There is no doubt that the computer does promote talk in ways which have hitherto been either difficult or impossible to arrange, but the effects of the computer on talking and listening are not yet completely understood: how much effect, for example, does a computer-managed task have on pupils when compared with other teaching strategies and does it alter the language experience or merely give it a different emphasis? Oracy has been a neglected part of the Language Arts curriculum for too long – perhaps it may be one of the greatest contributions of the computer that it will cease to be so.

5

RESEARCHING

*To live effectively is to live with
adequate information
(Norman Wiener, The Human
Use of Human Beings)*

A teacher wrote to me recently and stated that he could see little use for information-retrieval systems in the teaching of English, a view shared, I would think, by many teachers, especially those in the secondary sector. This view is engendered, I am sure, because information retrieval may not seem to have much relevance to what most teachers of English are attempting to do. Yet we live in an information society, a fact shown by the figures that Chandler (1982) cites, which show that in the USA in 1880, 45 per cent of the work-force was employed in agriculture and only 5 per cent in information-related industry. By 1980, those figures had changed dramatically, with only 2 per cent employed in agriculture and 47 per cent employed in the information industry. It is not relevant here to discuss the many reasons why this has happened, but one of the most obvious factors must be the development of rapid communications and the wide use of computer-related technology in that field. We are witnessing what has been called an 'information revolution', which has important consequences for our pupils. Already, we can see how the storage of information on computers is having an effect on our lives with bills, police records, social security, tax and banking information all being computerized. Less subtly, there are a number of existing computerized-information systems available to the public, both nationally and locally. Teletext, the television-based information system run by the IBA and BBC respectively under the names ORACLE and CEEFAX, was virtually unknown to my 12-year-old pupils two years ago, but last year (1984), over 70 per cent of them had television sets which could use the service. PRESTEL, the British Telecom information service to which access is gained via the telephone lines, has over 300,000 'pages' of information which are used, on average, over 15,000,000 times a month. In addition, and as a sign, perhaps, of things to come, the town where I live, Milton Keynes, started a local information system in October 1984 with a small number of terminals available for public use: one terminal, in the main shopping centre, was used 42,000 times in the first two weeks. Clearly, access to information is not only becoming easier, it is becoming a way of life, but a way of life that is new and demanding. As Adams and Jones put it:

> When so much information is at our disposal – and the volume seems likely to grow exponentially over the coming years – then it becomes increasingly important that we know how to handle these systems. How else can we keep any kind of control over our own lives and fashion the community that enables our full human development? To be cut off from the electronic sources of information will, indeed, render us powerless.
>
> (Adams and Jones, 1983, 48)

Concern with such considerations has led to the notion of 'information skills' which has, in turn, led to courses being developed in schools which purport to transmit these skills to the pupils. The courses often involve a description of information systems, their composition and use, and treat the concept as if it were accessible to the same teaching methods as transmitting the skills of paper-hat making: 'This is how you do it – now you know.' I would say that this is akin to ensuring that a child can read and then expecting him to be able to understand Shakespeare unaided. Once again, the belief in easily measurable and objective skills is undermining an important area of study for our pupils, an area which, for a full and deep understanding, demands involvement in processes rather than mastery of particular skills. Chandler makes this point most strongly when he states that:

> guided tours of someone else's frame of reference are not enough. Children are seldom allowed to contribute to [information systems], still less accorded equal priority. If we do not want them to grow up as the alienated consumers of chickfeed provided by the information rich then we must give them tools with which to create their own systems for sharing information with each other. And if we are to ensure that self-generated [information systems] are to become serious educational aids then we must surely make them available from the earliest possible age.
>
> (Chandler, 1984, 48)

His insistence on the involvement of the young and the sharing of information is important, because, as we shall see, using national databases does cost money and there is a real possibility that the state of a person's finances may determine the quantity and/or quality of information available to him. If the machinery for obtaining information becomes cheaper, as it almost certainly will in real terms, then profits will no doubt be sought from the information itself: there are already pages on PRESTEL which carry a charge – you must pay each time you look at the information on the page. The use of information systems in schools might be the only way that some children will ever get to learn about them.

There are other types of information systems, however, and these provide a way of involving the pupils in the compiling and use of information in a manner which PRESTEL, ORACLE and CEEFAX cannot. A program such as QUEST, available for both the BBC and RML computers, enables pupils to construct their own database and then 'interrogate' it in various ways in order to draw conclusions from the data: activities which should interest teachers of the Language Arts because of the language element implicit in such work. As we shall see, programs such as QUEST and VIEWDATA, when used imaginatively, can prove to be very useful aids indeed.

The message is, I hope, clear – we must give our pupils practical experience in the creation and usage of information systems if we are to equip them with the understanding necessary to cope with the demands which will be made on them.

Databases

I have mentioned a few information systems, but, in order to see how they relate to the classroom situation, it would be useful to explain how they operate (see Figure 4).

A database can be defined as information stored on a computer and national databases, such as ORACLE and CEEFAX, will contain information which will appeal to relatively large groups of people, such as the latest news and weather. Local databases are not necessarily local in the geographical sense, but are those to which there is limited access and which will probably contain information on a smaller range of subjects. In fact, there is a blurring of this distinction, for it is possible to incorporate information from national databases directly into local ones, as will be discussed later.

The most important difference between the two, however, is in the equipment required to have access to the databases. PRESTEL has over 300,000 'pages' (screenfuls of information) and is winning worldwide recognition as the pattern for other such systems. The information contained in the database is compiled not, for the most part, by PRESTEL but by organizations or firms which rent a number of pages collating and editing information in their own interest areas: these are called Information Providers (IPs). In order to use the database, one

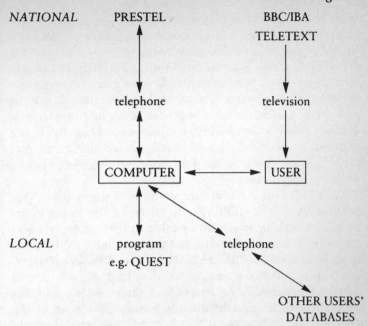

Figure 4 Databases: the flow of information

must either have a special PRESTEL handset or a computer which is then linked to the telephone line by a 'box of tricks' called a 'modem'. The modem enables the users' computer to be directly linked via the telephone line to one of a number of large computers sited around the country which contain the database.

The costs of using PRESTEL are therefore made up of the purchase of appropriate software, a modem – around £100 for the BBC and RML computers – telephone charges for the duration of the call and any charges incurred by looking at some frames of PRESTEL for which a fee is charged. A new educational package was announced in January 1985 for a limited period which reduced the cost, but it is worth knowing that the telephone line you intend using for PRESTEL access should be as direct as possible and, in some cases, may require a line to itself as any interference on the line, such as may be produced by some switchboards, can result in a broken connection, which is infuriating if it happens frequently. It is a good idea, therefore, to seek some advice about cost and suitability of the existing telephone arrangements before purchasing a modem.

PRESTEL does have a number of advantages over other national databases. CEEFAX and ORACLE, for example, are broadcast with the television signal and are therefore one-way communication, which restricts their usefulness in the classroom setting, unlike PRESTEL, which has a number of interactive features, such as a message-sending facility. They do only require the purchase or rental of a television set with the decoder, however, and there are no further costs incurred. It is also possible to link the BBC micro to Teletext and receive software (Telesoftware) which, in some cases, links directly with television programmes – a facility which has hardly been explored yet. It is interesting to note, however, that the Oxford Local Delegacy used CEEFAX Telesoftware in 1985 to distribute a program for GCE examination entries and made a slight reduction in entry fees for schools which submitted entries on a computer disc using this program. Teletext's greatest disadvantage is that it is limited to a few hundred pages of information, as compared to PRESTEL's 300,000, and that its information is geared far more to a general audience and has little space for specialist subjects.

A local database contains whatever information the user wishes it to contain, from a shopping list to census data from 100 years ago. All one needs to use it is a computer and the appropriate software. Of course, the major difference between national databases and local ones is that, with the latter, one needs (in most cases) actually to compile the information to be contained in it and enter this on the computer, which can be a very long and tedious task, but which can bring benefits for the teacher, as we shall see later. One recent development which could transform local database use, and, in a sense, make it more 'national', is the ability to send data via a telephone line to another user with the correct equipment – bringing extra costs, but another dimension. Chandler cites the case of a Californian research psychologist who created a Children's News Service linking children in an Eskimo village with pupils at a school in California:

> Each month the children, between nine and eleven years old, produce a newspaper together using their computers and an 'electronic mail' system. . . . The direct link between children living very different lives provides a real challenge. . . . In Dr. Levin's words, the Children's News Service allows young writers to 'get past the stage of writing as a mechanical act to writing as a communicative act.'
>
> (Chandler, 1984, 29)

The benefits of such an exercise are obvious even when the users are closer in culture; they are brought about simply by the ability to transmit data. Of course, one does not necessarily need to transmit data via a telephone line: an exchange of computer discs via the postal system can serve just as well.

Some of the latest local database software simulates PRESTEL both in presentation and in structure and has the added advantage that it is possible to 'download', or copy on to the computer, pages from the database, so that 'home-made' pages can be intermingled with ones from PRESTEL, thus blurring, to a certain extent, some of the differences between national and local databases. The structure of these systems, because of their potential size, can be a little complicated. The first page after the 'Welcome' page is an index or 'menu', which will direct the user to other indexes which, in turn, lead to pages of information about the chosen subject. Figure 5 may help to explain how this works. Note that the page numbers do not need to be typed: it is possible to set up 'routes' which require the pressing of only one number, obviating the need to have a complicated printed index of all the pages available and selecting them by 'name'. These 'routes' mean that it is possible to guide users, in the most painless way, around the database to the information they require. To someone who has not used this type of system before, it may seem difficult to understand, but pupils cope easily after only a brief introduction.

All the systems I have written about so far are based on prepared pages within a database using graphics as well as writing or figures, but there is another type, where the information is stored on the computer 'raw' or unprocessed and the user must ask questions to retrieve data, which is then ordered for display to the user. FACTFILE was an early attempt to use databases in education and demonstrates well this type of program. When a database is to be set up, the computer prompts the user to supply a number of headings for the data to be entered: for example, if the database were to be about pets, the headings might be 'Coat', 'Food', 'Noise', 'Habitat' and 'Qualities'. The computer then asks for the first pet and entries must be made for each heading in turn, such as 'Furry', 'Meat', 'Purr', 'Wherever it likes' and 'A pest'. This continues until the database is as complete as the user wishes, although it may be discovered in compiling the entries that some of the headings are inadequate and need to be modified. When the database is complete, other users can then consult it and are asked whether they wish to see the information about all the pets, one pet or ask for details under a specific heading. If they request the latter, they will be asked how many headings they wish to look at and the conditions which they wish to be met. In our example, the user may wish to look at all the entries which match the condition that 'Coat' is 'Furry' and 'Food' is 'Meat'. The program will then display in alphabetical order those pets

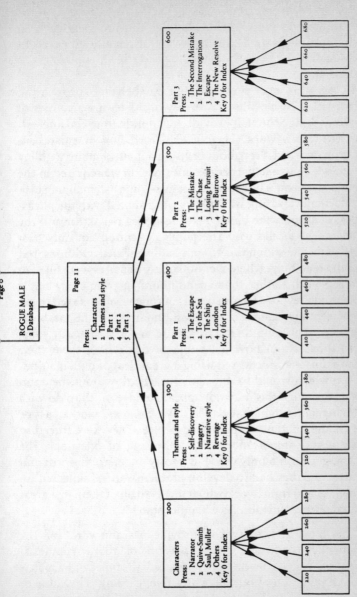

Figure 5 Example of the structure of a VIEWDATA database

The following text appears within the figure:

ROGUE MALE
a Database

Page 11

Press:
1 Characters
2 Themes and style
3 Part 1
4 Part 2
5 Part 3

200 — Characters

Characters
Press:
1 Narrator
2 Quive-Smith
3 Saul, Muller
4 Others
Key 0 for Index

210   240   260   280

300 — Themes and style

Themes and style
Press:
1 Self-discovery
2 Imagery
3 Narrative style
4 Revenge
Key 0 for Index

320   340   360   380

400 — Part 1

Part 1
Press:
1 The Escape
2 To the Sea
3 The Ship
4 London
Key 0 for Index

420   440   460   480

500 — Part 2

Part 2
Press:
1 The Mistake
2 The Chase
3 Losing Pursuit
4 The Burrow
Key 0 for Index

520   540   560   580

600 — Part 3

Part 3
Press:
1 The Second Mistake
2 The Interrogation
3 Escape
4 The New Resolve
Key 0 for Index

610   640   660   680

which are furry meat-eaters. Although this program has been superseded by more flexible software, it remains an excellent introduction to the use of databases and still has a place in the classroom.

I used a far more powerful, but cumbersome, program in 1984 with 12-year-olds in a survey of the leisure activities of pupils at Wing School. It provided an illuminating and interesting half-term's work. Having explained how the database program worked, I set about devising a questionnaire with my pupils which would gather the information we required in the form which would be the most useful – quite a demanding task intellectually and linguistically as we grappled with the phrasing of questions, the best type of response to ask for and the headings we would use. The pupils organized not only 'test runs' of the questionnaire, to spot badly phrased questions, but also the real thing, when over 600 questionnaires were filled in and returned. Rather than spend hours entering every single questionnaire – due to constraints of time – we managed to get a representative sample of the questionnaires into the database. We were then able to interrogate it and try to reach some conclusions about how the pupils at our school spent their leisure time – a process requiring a great deal of data manipulation, which would have been impractical without the computer. Although this may not appear to have much to do with the Language Arts at first glance, it was language work of a type the children had not experienced before. They were forced to examine the importance of the phrasing of questions, the meanings of commonly used but poorly understood words and phrases and they had to develop problem-solving skills within a small-group framework which involved all of them in a great deal of purposeful talk. As Chandler states:

> This kind of activity can provide a framework for the articulated exercise and extension of that hypothesis-making which goes on in our brains all the time, and which is the foundation of our most effective learning. The value of the activity as well as the 'validity' of its findings is dramati-

cally extended when it involves the sharing both of ideas and the business of investigation. Indeed it is in the languaging rather than in the use of the computer as such that the real learning takes place: enabling children to talk and write together about something far closer to 'research' than many of the activities which pass under that name in many schools.

(Chandler, 1984, 55)

I echo that statement wholeheartedly: nearly a year after the work was completed, pupils still mention it to me in discussion and, even if that is not a measure of the learning which took place, it is a demonstration of the impact such activities can have and which every teacher wishes could accompany all that they do in the classroom.

Class activities with databases

There are three main potential uses of databases in the classroom: as general databases, for newspapers and for work on books, although I have no doubt that imaginative teachers are discovering other uses. Each provides the basis for some interesting work and the possibility of linking with other disciplines in the school.

i) *General databases*

Constructing a database, as has been indicated above, is probably one of the best ways of using the computer as a research tool, no matter whether it contains raw or processed data. The collation of raw material for a database such as QUEST, however, can demand a large investment of time and needs careful planning, but do remember to include the pupils in that stage. It is very tempting to either make 'useful suggestions', which will have the effect of being an instruction, or to stop pupils making errors in order to save time, both of which should be avoided at all costs. Far better to allow the pupils to develop their own direction, mistakes and all, and discover their errors themselves. It is best to start, at least, by using a subject about which the pupils have direct experience, such as a survey of their classmates, local landmarks or the school itself, so that the data is not meaningless to them. It is also a good idea to include names the pupils will recognize, especially their own: when their name appears on the screen, it is almost as if they had just appeared on television!

Collecting the data can be the basis for useful discussions in itself, especially if it involves other people – pupils tend not to have much chance of conducting formal interviews in a real situation, and the experience is often a good learning opportunity. It is also very rewarding to involve other subject teachers in the collection of data, especially in the secondary school: apart from involving them in a computer-based project, their skills are frequently useful, particularly teachers from the maths department, who love a chance to show pupils the correct way to carry out calculations, and science teachers, whose insights into why, for example, Fred's feet are much bigger than David's can bring new dimensions and learning opportunities to the activity. Involving other subject areas has the added advantage of demonstrating to the pupils that language is not just confined to that subject labelled 'English' on the timetable, and that there are occasions when subject disciplines can be usefully combined.

Group work at this point is, of course, a must. It is particularly useful if there are as many headings as groups, but if this is impossible, it may be possible to subdivide the headings and organize subject-heading committees to cross-reference, analyse and collate the findings of the smaller groups. The management problem can be eased if other departments or teachers are involved, but, in any case, I found fairly regular, whole-group reporting-back sessions very important so that the pupils did not lose sight of the overall objective, a distinct danger if the groups are kept separate and the collection takes a long time. Such sessions act as a check to the whole procedure, for both the teacher and the pupils, and some errors in planning are easily detected in this way. I found it useful, too, to develop 'shopping lists' with each group during a reporting-back session, which detailed what they hoped to achieve before the next meeting, as this aided their planning and helped keep them 'on track'.

The final collation and entering of the data into the computer can be tedious and require many hours' work, but I found many willing volunteers to spend lunchtimes typing away, which, incidentally, acts as a good practice session of keyboard skills. However, this is one occasion where one must accept the inevitable and be prepared to do at least some of the donkey work oneself. It is worthwhile to ask each group to enter the data they collect under their own heading, if possible, because the raw material is often difficult for anyone else to read, and mistakes can occur. While this is going on, the rest of the group can usefully occupy their time by hypothesizing on what results they expect and why, and in framing the most effective questions to ask the database in order to check their theories. I discovered this the hard way, because I did not do it originally, and we wasted quite a lot of time as the groups formulated their research questions, with the computer ready and idle – an attraction which distracted some of the pupils from their task and set some groups off to the computer with half-baked ideas rather than a clear notion of what they were looking for.

Having set up the database, the teacher does need to provide some guidance as to the directions the research can take. If possible, of course, the groups should develop their own lines of enquiry and I found the simple question 'Why?' very useful indeed in setting them off in a particular direction. The purpose of the exercise was something which had to be made very clear from the outset, because, as with all classroom activities, the pupils work best if they know why they're doing something. My rationale for the survey was to produce a report on its results (which they would write) which would prove whether or not, as many teachers claimed, they did nothing with their spare time, the original starting point of the whole exercise. As with all good intentions, however, we were side-tracked and the report was never written, although that did not devalue the exercise in any way in the eyes of the pupils — end results aren't always tangible.

ii) Newspapers

It has long been the practice of Language Arts teachers to use the production of a newspaper as a method of creating a purposeful framework for writing, as well as a means of understanding newspapers as a medium. However, with the advent of public databases and the apparent demand for Teletext and PRESTEL, the possibility of an electronic newspaper is not far off — indeed, some would say that it has already arrived, with a number of computer magazines being published on cassette for use with particular microcomputers. The PRESTEL format lends itself to use in this way, with story-sized pages and the possibility of rudimentary graphics, and programs such as INFOFILE for the BBC are beginning to be heavily marketed because they provide the facility for copying pages from PRESTEL as well as acting as a local Viewdata system.

The structure of these types of databases lends itself to the production of a newspaper because it is split into different sections with their own indexes. It is possible, therefore, to envisage small groups in the classroom working on sections of the newspaper with an editorial team having the final decision on which stories are to appear in each issue. The beauty of this way of producing a newspaper is that it is very easy to erase a page and insert another, unlike the traditional pen-and-paper approach, which depended upon children writing, or typing out, their stories. The resulting newspaper looked like anything but a newspaper, unless one spent time and had the reprographics facilities available to present an acceptable facsimile. INFOFILE, and other programs like it, now produce a professional-looking 'newspaper', because it uses the same graphics and lettering as PRESTEL and the Teletext services. It is possible to print out the pages (although not all printers will manage the pictures), so a copy can be obtained for each pupil without too much effort.

A program released by Suffolk Educational Software early in 1985, called DATAVIEW, simulates a Teletext-style database, rather than the Viewdata type, and could be regarded as a 'gentle' introduction to the more complicated databases (although it is no less sophisticated in presentation), because the sometimes rather complex 'routing' procedure necessary with the creation of a Viewdata database is not needed. Each page is given a number and in order to see that page its number must be used – thus demanding the inclusion of a complete index, or series of indexes, in the database. Pages can be 'linked' by a very simple procedure, however, so that the user can 'browse' through the database, in an order defined by the creator, merely by pressing the space bar. An added feature is the ability to display each page in turn for a selected period of time without anyone pressing any keys – the way to display the database/newspaper in the library or on parents' evenings, perhaps.

In terms of organization, small groups of pupils can be assigned to each section of the newspaper, with the resulting discussion about the sections of a newspaper and their usual contents, and be assigned to cover particular stories. I feel that it is always good to start with something which the pupils have experience of and, as has been stated above, they love to see their names, and those of their friends, on screen. Local stories are probably the best to start with, therefore, and the most obvious stories concern the school sports teams and items of news around the school. One group should be assigned to the editorial section with the power of veto over any story, although the teacher should, sensibly, have the final say in delicate stories which might mention, for example, particular people in a less than flattering light. Exercising this power without using a heavy hand is difficult, but it is an interesting way to start a discussion about defamation of character and censorship! The groups' tasks should be rotated with each issue, to give everyone the chance to get each other back for rejecting their story when they were on the editorial board! I have found that the more realistic the setting, the more the pupils respond and the better the resulting work.

Displaying pupils' work should be a matter of course, and not just within the group. If they are to accept responsibility for what they write and if the exercise is to be real in any way, the work must be publicly displayed. The library appears to me to be an ideal place: apart from the fact that there will probably be other newspapers available, it will encourage the writers to understand more clearly what having an audience means, particularly if there is a 'Reader's Response' page which allows for comments to be made on stories and for letters to the editor. This last idea has the advantage that, fairly soon, millions of people, rather than the present thousands who use PRESTEL for that purpose, will have an electronic mail service readily available and the electronic newspaper in the library will help prepare pupils for its wider use.

iii) Work from books

As I mentioned in Chapter 3, some programs became available in 1984 which, amidst massive pressure marketing, were announced as study aids to accompany some major classics, including Shakespeare. I have already stated that I feel them to be a little misguided in their claims that the 'answers' are given – the suggestion of certain scenes containing particular themes, for example, may give the user the idea that no other scenes contain appropriate references. However, the idea behind these programs does seem to contain a great deal of potential for use in the classroom: imagine the work which could arise out of the pupils building a database on a book they had been reading. It is a great pity that the company which produced the study aids did not sell the program as a structure, ready for teachers to use it with whichever book they wished. No doubt someone will realize the potential of such a program and one will become available designed for teachers, rather than for the more lucrative home market.

Nevertheless, it is possible to adapt a number of database programs, such as QUEST and, even, INFOFILE, to this purpose. There are, as I see it, a number of ways in which this could be organized. One could have a database on the whole book, with various groups of pupils working on characters, events, and themes, as well as on background material (see, for example, Figure 5, page 83). At the start, the group would decide the headings that are going to be used in the database and then work within their groups on finding information from the book to place under the headings. On the other hand, there could be a number of databases on the same book, each dealing with one aspect of it, but this might require some complicated cross-referencing – not, I am sure, beyond some pupils, particularly if they have experience of databases. It does depend, of course, on the ability of the pupils, but it would be a new approach to studying books and would certainly encourage pupils to engage in reflective reading.

On the other side of the coin, the use of a carefully structured database would allow for some interesting hypothesis-making and -testing in a manner which would otherwise be more difficult. A pupil studying *Rogue Male*, for example, would be able to cross-reference a character trait of the Narrator with specific incidents in the book, or the pupil reading *The Silver Sword* would be able to see how the children reacted to particular incidents for a comparison between them. It might be argued that pupils can do this anyway, if they are prepared actually to flick the pages. However, I am not arguing for this as a *replacement* for the more traditional methods, but as an additional method to use, which may, of course, have more appeal for children if they have not yet developed sufficient skill to search, or are resistant to searching, a text for references.

CONCLUSIONS

Far from detracting from the work of Language Arts teachers, the use of databases can be a positive aid in developing children's language abilities, but they must be involved in processes rather than, as Chandler puts it, taking part in 'guided tours of someone else's frame of reference'. Much work needs to be done to develop this relatively new area of exploitation of the computer in education, but programs already exist which provide a starting point for teachers on which to base their demands for the contents of those programs which will, without any doubt, appear over the next few years. These programs offer the opportunity for language work to spill out of the lessons marked 'English' on the timetable and encompass other subject disciplines in a way which has not been possible in the past. Language Arts teachers should, I believe, take the initiative and use databases as one means to help pupils become autonomous learners.

PART TWO:
THE PRACTICAL ASPECTS

6

CLASSROOM MANAGEMENT

I tell you, sir, the only safeguard of order and discipline in the
modern world is a standardized worker with interchangeable
parts. That would solve the entire problem of management.
(Giraudoux, *The Madwoman of Chaillot*)

In previous chapters I have been concentrating on the various
aspects of the Language Arts and attempting to show how the
computer can be used in a variety of ways to enhance the
teaching of these elements, but I have said little, as yet, about
the practical 'nuts and bolts' of how to actually use the
computer in the classroom and the considerations which must
be taken into account before using it for the first time. I intend,
in this chapter, to discuss the practical problems, but a word of
warning is, I think, apposite: we are all different. That may not
seem a terribly staggering point to make, but, as various
researchers have shown, teaching styles are very difficult to
quantify or, some would say, identify at all, so the following
discussion should not be seen as prescriptive, merely as an
introduction and starting point for further thought. It is important to realize that, just as there is no formula for good
teaching, so there is no pattern which will guarantee success
with the use of computers in teaching. There are, however,
useful guidelines for good teaching, and I hope that I can offer
at least some guidelines which will help teachers using com-

puters for the first time to ensure that their first experiences with the computer will not put them off for life.

Using a computer in one's teaching should not be a hit-and-miss affair – after all, one would not just pick any old book from the shelf and, without reading it, use it as a class reader. Similarly, the use of the computer in the Language Arts should be a departmental decision if possible, as policy issues are involved. The whole process, from choosing which computer to use to where it plugs in, is a complex matter and a policy across a department will not only aid the teachers, but also help the children to have a consistent experience. In fact, I would argue that a policy needs to be developed within each school, so that 'computer literacy' is a school-based concept rather than just department-based (see Chapter 8).

Which computer?

Let us begin, then, at the first stage: that of choosing a computer. I shall leave it to others to discuss the technical aspects of different computers because for most teachers the two operative criteria are cost and software availability. In some cases, there will be little or no choice in which computer to buy, as a number of education authorities have a particular policy on one machine. The policy will normally relate to computers bought out of the school's capitation allowance, so funds from PTAs and other sources account for some computers that do not come within the county policy being provided in schools. Other authorities do have a freer policy, allowing the purchase of whichever computer the school feels suits their purposes. This has resulted in a rather confused picture over the country as a whole, with some schools possessing computers of varying makes and others with only one type of computer. This was exacerbated to a certain extent by the original Department of Industry's offer to schools over the past few years, which gave its 'seal of approval' to three makes of computer: the BBC B, the Sinclair

Spectrum and the Research Machines 380 and 480Z, and enabled schools to buy one of them, in effect, at half price. A fairly recent, but small, survey gave some interesting results which show how this is reflected in schools:

Machines	% Owning	
	Primary	Secondary
RML 380Z	4	62
RML 480Z	19	17
BBC B	73	78
ZX Spectrum	14	18

(*Educational Computing*, June 1984)

In this extract from the survey, I have indicated only those machines which formed part of the DI offers, but it is clear that the BBC computer has taken the 'lion's share' of the school market so far. The reasons for this can only be speculated upon, but I am convinced that it has a lot to do with price. The BBC computer, with a retail price of about £300, was a reasonable buy as a home computer, whereas the Research Machine 480Z, with a list price of about £400, is not, despite the fact that it has a 64K memory, as opposed to the BBC's 32K, and computer programs are beginning to require large memories. It does seem a reasonably useful facility for a school to have a computer which, very possibly, the pupils also have at home. This would seem to indicate that the Spectrum, a computer with a bigger memory than the BBC B, would be the natural choice, as its list price is only about £100, but it has a non-standard keyboard – that is, although the keys have the same QWERTY arrangement, they also have other functions and they are the rubberpad type, which does not help keyboard-skill development as much as a conventional moving-key keyboard. Educational discounts are available, of course, and the removal of VAT for educational establishments does mean that, although they keep the same price differential, they are much cheaper. However, as the BBC B remains the cheapest computer with a standard keyboard, it would appear that it is the best value for money.

This, until recently, has been justified further by the availability of good quality software. Anyone who has had an RML computer for a number of years will not need telling that there has been a great paucity of software for the Humanities subjects. As I have indicated throughout this book, however, more programs are becoming available which are easing the situation somewhat. Nevertheless, the BBC B, with its position as a good-selling home computer, does appear to have the edge over the RMLs. The latest Acorn brochure, with programs for the BBC B computer, contains programs marketed in schools as well as on the home market, and some of them are of high educational quality. It is probable, therefore, that until RML prices are reduced, the BBC computer will continue to take a large share of the market.

However, a sixteen-station RML network has been provided by Staffordshire for every high school in the county, and there is little doubt that RML have begun to 'swing the tide' somewhat by their concentration on networking, that is, the ability to link computers together. The system is called an 'upgrade path' and starts with the purchase of a single 480Z computer using a cassette. This computer can then be 'upgraded' to work from a disc drive (see below for a discussion of this) which can serve a number of computers. Having developed a number of computers being served from the 'shared-disc' system, the purchase of a Network Server will enable all of the computers to work either on the network or as 'stand-alone' machines. Schools can thus enlarge their computer provision as they can afford it. The BBC computer's alternative is called Econet, which allows computers to be linked in a similar way, but it is not possible to operate the BBCs as 'stand-alone' machines operating from one disc drive in the same way as the RML system.

Having said that, 1985 is seeing some changes in the computers available. In January, Research Machines announced a new computer called the Nimbus which, although more expensive than the 480Z as a stand-alone machine, compares fairly favourably in cost as a network facility. The Nimbus is not just an updated 480Z, however, it is what is called a 'sixteen-bit' computer, which means that, not only is the memory size increased considerably, but its speed of operation is also much better. Unfortunately, the software for the 480Z is not automatically compatible with the Nimbus, but, to be honest, if the Nimbus's potential is realized in new software, it will leave 480Z software far behind in terms of presentation and capabilities: it represents what could be termed 'the next generation' of home and educational computers. Developments happen so quickly in computing that, by the time this book is published, it may well be that even this machine is out of date: the new BBC computer is due for launch as I write, and this could have an equally important impact on education.

The whole subject is a complex one and very careful investigations are necessary before embarking on the purchase of computers, but one criteria must apply – the use to which the computer is to be put. It would not be sensible, needless to say, to buy a computer which is not appropriate for its use: for example, it would not be wise to buy a computer for its networking facilities if there is no likelihood of a network system ever being needed, nor would it be sensible to buy a computer which is restricted in memory size if the programs one wanted to use demanded a bigger memory. I will not, therefore, state which computer is the best to buy – ultimately, the choice will depend upon a great many variables.

CASSETTE OR DISC?

The question of whether one should use a disc-based or a cassette-based system is easier to answer than deciding which computer to buy. Computers have a memory area inside them (it might be easier to consider this as a blank page) into which the programs one buys are loaded. The programs themselves can be stored in a number of ways, including cassettes and discs. Programs stored on a cassette are in the form of audio signals, which are converted inside the computer into computer-recognizable form and then stored in the appropriate memory area – the RAM (Random Access Memory) but not, however, the ROM (Read Only Memory), which has memory areas that contain essential operating instructions for the computer and which can be altered only in certain circumstances. Disc-based programs are stored on a disc which is rather like a small audio record in a stiff paper carrier. When put into a disc drive, the disc is 'read' by magnetic read/write heads, a little like cassette players in principle. This simplistic explanation of the difference between cassette and disc does not include the most significant one – speed of loading. With a cassette-based system, loading times of five minutes are not uncommon, depending upon the size of the program – the longer and more complex the program, the longer it takes to load. A similar program, when loaded from disc, will have a loading time measured in seconds. With all the other problems facing a teacher using the computer in the classroom, waiting for five minutes for a program to be loaded before it can even be used is very frequently frustrating, to say the least.

What is even worse, many programs enable work to be 'saved' – stored for future use or reference – and the time taken to save anything is correspondingly longer with cassette. If one wishes to check that the work has been saved without errors, it is necessary to rewind the tape and reload or verify the data by means of a 'verify' command to the computer. Most disc systems check what they are saving as they do it and those which do not take only seconds to check. Finding the right place on the cassette tape can be a problem, too, as the only indication that one has as to where a particular program starts is often the tape counter, which, if it is not zeroed at the start of the session and a careful note taken of the number when the data is stored, can have the user tearing his hair out. Discs do not have this problem, as the data is stored wherever there is space on the disc and an internal operating system will tell the computer exactly where it is, thus obviating the need to record numbers.

For these reasons, and others which will become apparent, I would consider anyone purchasing a computer without a disc drive as being foolish in the extreme, unless there are financial reasons why this is not possible. Discs are, without doubt, the most efficient storage medium of the alternatives discussed so far and the sooner cassette-based systems disappear from schools the better.

Two other methods of storing programs, but not pupils' work, are worth mentioning, as their use is beginning to become more widespread. One is a ROM-pack, a little box which connects directly into a socket provided on most computers. I have already mentioned that ROM stands for Read Only Memory and is the type of memory which one cannot normally use because it contains operating instructions for the computer. These packs, when inserted, become part of the operating system of the computer and, because of the way the computer works, the program is loaded almost instantly: thus it is a much quicker way of loading programs than discs. However, one cannot save data on the ROM-packs, so they are not a replacement for the other methods. Similarly, it is possible to buy some programs on silicon chips, which one fits to the insides of the computer. The thought of tampering with the insides of a computer may fill some with horror, but these chips really are easy to fit. The most commonly used program available in chip form is WORDWISE, a word processor for the BBC computer, and hundreds of these have been fitted by complete novices without mishap. As with the ROM-pack, the program is loaded almost instantly and can be switched on or off very simply and quickly.

OTHER PERIPHERALS

As will now be obvious, buying a computer means buying more than just the computer itself, and one should not take a basic price quoted by a manufacturer as the total price when purchasing a complete system. The 'other bits' which are necessary are called peripherals, but are far from incidental in importance.

The usual way a computer communicates with the user is through what is often called a VDU – a Visual Display Unit, or, to put that in English, a television set or monitor. The difference between a television set and a monitor may seem unimportant until one actually sees computer output displayed on both. All computers have a socket for a normal UHF connector, the sort used with domestic television sets. This carries a signal which is decoded inside the television to produce the picture on the screen. The signal from a computer is different in a number of ways but, to put it simply, does not need to go through the same decoding procedure inside a television set. Using a monitor will therefore result in a sharper, much 'cleaner' picture than through a television screen, which is very much an advantage if the program uses graphics, as many do. For that purpose, the computer will have at least one more output socket specifically for a monitor. In fact, there are now television/monitors available which can perform both functions – an alternative for schools where resources are limited. The fact that there are at least two outputs for a VDU on most computers can be a useful feature, because, of course, the picture being transmitted is the same whichever socket is being used and both can be used at the same time, although it should be noted that the display on the VDU connected by the ordinary coaxial cable will be in black and white only with most computers. In order to run more than one monitor from one computer, look for an electronics enthusiast who will make a 'signal splitter', that is, a box with one input, from the computer, and two outputs, for two monitors. However, this is rather a Heath Robinson approach and if the cables are too long the signal may break up. Nevertheless, it is possible to run two VDUs at once, ensuring that, whatever the circumstances, all members of a group should be able to see the display.

I have indicated elsewhere that, for use in the Language Arts especially, the facility to obtain a 'hard copy' – a printed record – is a very useful feature. In order to do this, a printer will be needed, which, again, can be connected to most computers with little difficulty. There are various types of printer available, the price depending upon the quality and range of printing possible. It is important to check which type of printer is compatible with the computer being bought: not every printer will necessarily work with every type of computer, because there are two ways – called 'serial' or 'parallel', which use different connectors – in which information is transmitted by a computer to a printer. There are adapters available to convert one type of signal to the other, but this is an extra expense for schools where resources are limited.

The basic configuration is, therefore, computer – disc drive (or cassette-player) – monitor/television – printer, as well as the leads necessary for connecting it all together, and, incidentally, the leads can prove more expensive than one might think. There are other peripherals one can use, however, such as Concept Keyboards, Microwriters and Mouses (not a grammatical error!) which I will deal with later, as they will, in all probability, not figure in the initial considerations about purchasing a computer system.

Where will it be kept?

An important aspect which should be considered before the purchase of a computer, if possible, is storage. Unfortunately, one of the more important factors is security, because the computer itself will be extremely portable and, thus, easy to steal. If the computer is going to be used by the pupils, knowledge of where it is kept will be widely available, no matter how hard one may try to keep it a secret! In one school I know of, this aspect has been taken to extremes, with the school computers being kept inside a locked box inside a locked store cupboard inside a locked room: the computer is so safe that no teachers use it at all! On the other hand, keeping the computer open to public view with no attempt to secure it acts as an invitation to some people. Clearly, some sensible precautions will not go amiss, such as keeping the computer in a room which is not on the ground floor, bolting it to a stand or on a computer trolley, and covering it with the name of the school in ultra-violet pen, but the security angle must be balanced with accessibility, both for teachers and pupils. Ideally, it must be secure but it should not take the teacher half an hour to locate and set up the computer in order to use it.

One alternative is to create a 'computer room', where all computers are kept: if the room can be made secure, the computers need not be bolted down. However, there are some wider implications for this arrangement which need careful consideration. In the first place, if the computers are going to be set up in a computer room, with no possibility of moving them for use in classrooms, the problem of booking the facility is raised. Either one must allow teachers to book the room as they wish or the room must be allocated between the teachers so that access is restricted to a particular teacher at a certain time or times. In the former case, there is the possibility of teachers being able to gain access to the room when they need to use the computers, but only if someone has not booked it first and, in the latter, not every teacher will need to use it at their allotted time. Other subjects may be able to identify a need to use the computer for specific purposes at specific times, but computer use in the Language Arts will rarely be that predictable.

Secondly, a room full of computers, in all likelihood networked, may seem an attractive possibility to the many people who consider that one computer between thirty pupils is unworkable. Yet, apart from the fallacy of that view (see page 127), the times are few when all that one needs when working with the computer is just the computer itself: there will be other resources necessary to the exercise which must be set up in the computer room, and the time seen as being saved by not having to collect the computer and connect it up can be spent in organizing the other resources in the computer room. When the computer is in the classroom, all the resources in the classroom are available with little effort and the computer becomes just one more resource amongst many, as opposed to being the focal point of the room, which could give the computer greater importance than the activity for which it is being used, in the eyes of the pupils.

On the other hand, if the computers are kept in different places the useful networking facility could be lost, unless the network cables were run around the school, and that could prove not only very difficult in some cases, but probably very expensive. In addition, the physical layout of the school can present problems with the movement of computers, which would be necessary if there were not enough for one per classroom. As mentioned above, there will probably be a number of items to transport – computer, disc drive, monitor, printer – some of which are relatively fragile, and the possibilities of damage occurring are far greater than with a computer room facility. There is a further likelihood of damage if there are stairs to negotiate or if the movement entails going between buildings: it is best to avoid subjecting computers and their peripherals to the vicissitudes of the weather and rapid changes in temperature. It is, of course, possible to buy trolleys designed for computers – which double as 'work stations' – these have the advantage that the whole system can be connected up permanently, apart from the mains plugs, thus saving time.

In an ideal world, it would be possible to develop a system which has the best elements of both: where there is a computer room full of computers on moveable, lockable trolleys which can be taken to classrooms wired for several computers to be linked into a network both within the classroom and over the whole school. Unfortunately, this is not within the resources of most schools, so a compromise must be reached. The local conditions will dictate the parameters of the solution, but a whole-school policy is desirable at the outset, rather than as a later attempt to rationalize a piecemeal buying policy.

Initial staff training

Once the computer arrives in the department, there is a great deal to be done before it can be used in the classroom and, unfortunately, this takes time. I make this point because it seems that there are a number of people who are keen to start using new resources as soon as they arrive. This may be the case more particularly with a computer, which will probably arrive after a great deal of discussion and expectation. There may also be the attention of other colleagues, which will add extra pressure, particularly if money has been diverted away from other areas of the school.

The first task is for everyone who will be using the computer to learn how to connect all the 'bits and pieces' together and this raises the phenomenon already being labelled 'technophobia'. There is no doubt that many people have absolutely no interest in machines of any kind and appear to have a complete mental block where any form of machinery is concerned. A few years ago, I was responsible for the introduction of a plain-paper copier into my school, which was available for general use. In order to obtain copies, all the user had to do was to press the button to set the machine to work and then the buttons labelled with numbers for the number of copies required. It was, at the time, a great surprise that a large number of staff were completely mystified by this and seemed incapable of operating what, to me, was an incredibly simple machine. I became somewhat irritated when I was asked to explain the operation of the copier to someone for the umpteenth time. One important thing to remember here is that many teachers did know how to use it once I had explained it, but when they were not using it very often, they forgot quite quickly. Frequent use does, without doubt, help to overcome such problems. With computers, however, the situation can be far worse and, for many teachers, they hold a terror unparalleled by even the worst imaginable class! I am sure that the computer has achieved a mystique in their minds far above any normal machine. Why this has happened is partly due, I am sure, to the 'hype' of advertisers and those who are wildly enthusiastic about computers. The fact that it happens at all contains a lesson which I believe is a valuable one: computers need to lose the aura being built around them. They are, after all, just machines, and it is quite difficult actually to damage one, short of throwing it on the ground. The best way to discover this is to 'play' with one, which is why I suggest that as soon as possible after the computer has arrived, a departmental meeting is arranged, preferably with a computer 'expert' on call, where all members of the department have the opportunity to play with the computer before they learn how to put it together. There is no substitute for 'hands-on experience' when it comes to demystifying the computer and, just as there is a place for play in education, there is a definite place for play in in-service education for teachers. In fact, my first real experience with a computer was when the Computer Studies teacher left the school computer in the staff room during a summer term for teachers to use when they had 'non-teaching time'.

Eventually, however, the time must come when teachers must be trained in how to connect all the various parts together. This is important even if there is either a technician available or if the computer is left permanently set up. There is nothing worse than interrupting a lesson with its consequent disruption of pupils' attention and interest if all that is wrong with the computer is that one lead is not in the right place or has fallen out of its socket – especially, of course, if the lead has been 'helped' on its way by a pupil. It is a good idea, therefore, to 'colour code' or otherwise mark the leads and sockets, so that it is easy to see if a lead has been connected wrongly or come out of its socket. In any case, even if the teachers forget the initial training, it is one way of demystifying the computer and emphasizing its fallibilities.

Once teachers are familiar with the computer, the real in-service training can begin. As I have stated before, I believe that it is very important that the computer be integrated into a department's scheme of work rather than the other way around, so that a discussion of the issues involved should be high on the agenda, with the emphasis on what one is trying to achieve. In examining how the computer can be employed, it will soon become apparent that the computer is just a machine and that it is the software which is important. One weighty consideration, therefore, will be the evaluation of software.

SOFTWARE EVALUATION

Publishers are reluctant to provide an 'inspection copy' service to teachers when it comes to software, which is not surprising considering the relative ease with which it is possible to copy programs. This does make it difficult, however, because there is little doubt that the best way to evaluate a program is by actually using it on a computer, having the time to examine all its aspects. Therefore, before even considering how to evaluate software, it is necessary to obtain a copy of a program without committing oneself to purchasing it. Some local authorities, realizing the difficulties, have endeavoured to establish a software library – often in teachers' centres, where they exist – which is certainly useful. However, if a visit to such a centre involves a long journey, this may prove difficult for classroom teachers with all their other commitments, especially if it is by no means certain that their visit will prove fruitful. It would, perhaps, be idealistic to propose that teachers should be able to telephone their requirements to someone who would then bring a selection of programs to the school to be examined. Nevertheless, where a publisher already employs a representative to visit schools with selections of books, it might be a very good idea to lobby the representative to bring computer software as well. Another idea occurred to me when I saw a 'magazine' which is sold for a number of home computers in the form of a cassette-based computer program. This, when loaded into the computer, displays pages of text. In most of these types of magazines, there are 'reviews' of the latest games which include an extract from the game so that the reader can actually play parts of the game – the hope being that, having enjoyed playing part of the game without the possibility of copying all of it, the reader will then go out and purchase it. Perhaps software publishers could distribute 'sample' discs and tapes containing at least part of the program for teachers to try out.

One idea gaining some support in various areas around the country is for local authorities to obtain programs under licence upon payment of an appropriate fee. This enables the authority to distribute copies of the programs to schools under their jurisdiction at either a reduced cost, or free, depending upon the policy of the county in question. This appears to be an excellent arrangement, but it is too early yet to judge whether this will prove successful on a wide scale: as yet, it is available only from certain sources and for chosen software. It is worth checking, however, what licence agreements exist in the LEA and pressing for more.

Given the difficulty in obtaining review copies, magazines such as *Educational Computing* and *Computers In the Teaching of English* are useful in that they provide reviews of a selection of programs, the reviews in the latter publication being written by classroom teachers. Although these provide only 'second-hand' information, they can be a useful guide for the purchase of programs. In addition, it is quite a good idea to contact other schools in the locality to find out which programs they are using and, possibly, arrange a visit to see them 'in action'.

Having obtained a copy of a program, the next problem is to assess its worth. There have been a number of checklists published which can provide a good starting point for discussion or thought about the value of a program (see, for example, Chandler, 1984), but one should never buy one program simply because it gets more ticks on a checklist than another. The ultimate criterion should be whether the program fits the teachers' needs, and that will obviously depend upon the context in which it will be used.

There are three main areas of consideration: technical aspects, presentation and documentation. Of the three, probably the least important is documentation – that is, the booklets and materials which go with the program to explain its operation and suggest ways in which it might be used. Whatever documentation is provided with a program, I have always found that it is necessary to provide what are often referred to, rather unkindly, as 'idiot sheets', which give straightforward, step-by-step guides as to which buttons to press, and when. It would, therefore, be rather short-sighted to reject an otherwise excellent piece of software just because the documentation is poor. This cannot be said of the other two areas, however. The operation of a program should intrude as little as possible on the task demanded of the user: for example, complicated sequences of key-presses for necessary or frequently used facilities can be irritating, not to say distracting, for a pupil and should be avoided. Ideally, it should be possible for anyone, regardless of computer expertise, to use the program properly without getting into difficulties for which there is no on-screen guidance.

Evaluation skills are acquired with practice, of course, and within a relatively short time most teachers will be able to assess which programs are going to be useful and which are not. Having decided which software is going to be used, a consideration of the effects that using the computer in the classroom will have becomes important.

Power in the classroom

It is apparent that the teacher's role has changed subtly in the classroom, but in ways which can be most unsettling, especially for the experienced teacher. It has been noted that the teacher can become technician in certain circumstances, a role which will be nothing new to those who have struggled with recalcitrant video machines and the like. This is, it is true, an extension of the teacher's role, but it is of minor concern and consequence when compared to the alteration of the power structure within the classroom.

The first time that I used a computer in my teaching, I was aware that I was close to panic many times – not because the lesson was going badly, but because it was going well! It is amazing how compulsive a television screen is to pupils and adults alike: since the first few lessons with the computer, I have conducted a number of 'experiments', placing a television at various points around the classroom and noting the direction of the pupils' attention. In most cases, the blank screen attracted the pupils no matter what activity was being undertaken and the nearer it was to me, the more conscious I became that it was almost as if the pupils were superimposing my face on the television screen! I suppose that my lessons were more acceptable if they imagined that they were being forced to watch a television programme! In retrospect, therefore, I am not surprised that I felt near panic in my first lesson with the computer, because, not only was there the power of the television screen dominating the pupils' minds, but also the fascination that many children have with computers: in short, I felt that I was not in control of events. There is, of course, nothing more frightening for a teacher than the feeling that he is not in control, and the feeling of insecurity is immense. However, it is a fact that, despite our progress in teaching methods over the years, I still get the distinct impression that the volume of noise emanating from the classroom is seen as one measure of a teacher's control – in one school where I taught not so many years ago, there was a great deal of kudos in being able to keep the classroom door open and not disturb other classes. This added to my sense of insecurity with that first computer lesson, because I felt that someone was going to open the door and demand to know what was going on, although the lesson was only noisy in parts. In the end, it was while reflecting on what I would answer if that should happen that I realized what exactly had happened – I was not control-ling the activity, but I was in control of the situation: further, I was freed from the necessity of overseeing the activity and could do what I wanted to do: monitor the small groups working within the classroom. After that point, I gladly relin-quished the management of the activity to the computer and capitalized on the real power the computer gave me – to become a free agent, roaming the classroom and becoming an adviser, a devil's advocate, a *learner*.

The power structure of a lesson often has expression in the physical layout of a classroom – the raised dais at the front used to be more than just a way of seeing what was going on. The siting of the computer is therefore an important consideration and will probably result in some change to the existing arrange-ments. In deciding where the computer is put a number of points need to be taken into account. Firstly, the nature of the activity to be undertaken will determine the best position for the computer. If small groups are going to be working on it in rotation, it would be very distracting to place the computer and its screen in a position which would make the display easily seen by all the other pupils. If the activity is in any way competitive, this would give the others a chance to see what each group is doing, and would defeat the object of the exercise. Even if there is no competitive element, the mere visibility of the screen would prove distracting for those not using it or engaged in another activity, so it is best if the computer is placed in such a way that no one, other than the group working on it, can see the display. On the other hand, this would be clearly inappropriate if it was necessary for the whole group to watch the screen at once. This may seem a difficult management problem, but the answer to it lies in the second main consideration.

When the whole group is doing work with the computer at once – a group cloze exercise, for example – it is necessary for all of them to see the screen at once, which means that a normal 12- or 14-inch display screen will be inadequate. It is therefore most desirable to have available a large television set, or possibly a TV/monitor, for these situations. As mentioned earlier, most computers have at least two outputs for a visual display: a normal coaxial output and what is referred to as a TTL or RGB outlet. This is invaluable here, for not only can the computer be connected to a large television screen, for the group to watch, but it can also be connected to the small monitor for the teacher to use. Nothing is worse than typing something and having to crane one's neck in order to see the results – this also means that, just as with a blackboard, one's attention is diverted from the class. It should, therefore, be possible to place the computer permanently in the classroom so that the small monitor's display is invisible to the class, because, when the whole group needs to use it, the large television provides the display.

Thirdly, movement to and from the computer should cause the least fuss possible. It would be unwise to place the computer so that pupils have to move chairs and tables in order to get to it. Associated with this problem is the seemingly miles of wiring necessary to connect the different parts of the computer together. Apart from the safety aspect, ripping wires out of the computer by tripping over them can be costly and lose valuable work. It does seem that we are gradually working towards a wire-less environment (it is now possible to telephone Australia from the middle of a field), but until that time arrives, cables will be a problem in the classroom. It therefore makes sense to place the computer as close as possible to a power socket and against a wall, so that the wires can be 'hidden' against the wall with some form of shielding, even if they are only taped. In some schools, it is not unusual to have a 'paint' corner, or a book section, distinct from the rest of the classroom – in the same way, it should not be impossible to have a 'computer corner', although it may need some rearrangement.

Even if it is impossible to have a permanent facility in the classroom which takes all of these considerations into account, it is important to be aware of them and to try to create the most appropriate physical layout. If the computer is to be a powerful aid to learning, it must not be allowed to dominate the classroom and dictate the relationships within it. This is what is at the root of teacher insecurity when the computer is in the classroom, the feeling that one is 'handing over' part of the teacher's role to a machine. Yet, with the confidence which practice gives, and the attention to the positioning of the computer, it will become evident that all that is happening is that the teacher is relinquishing part of his/her control over events in order to become more of a participant in them.

KEYBOARD SKILLS

One of the problems which will be encountered by both teacher and pupils alike is the lack of practice in keyboard skills: that is the speed of typing and a general knowledge of how to communicate with the computer. Fortunately, this is likely to be a problem to be faced only in the short term, because those starting school now who have access to a computer at home and at school will develop keyboard skills from an early age, and typing at a keyboard will become as easy for some (if not easier) than writing with a pen. Nevertheless, there will probably always be those whose skills need practice and I would envisage a time when, just as we have special arrangements for those with difficulties in reading and writing, there will be classes for helping those with poor keyboard skills. In today's classroom, it is not only the pupils who need help: teachers may not have had much use of computers and most cannot type with any facility, so here is an added problem. For the teachers, this may not be a serious one although it is often more difficult to learn new skills as we grow older, but for the pupils this can become yet one more way in which it is possible to fail. There are pupils of mine who are very slow at typing and the disparaging comments from those more familiar with keyboards hurt just as much as comments about difficulty with reading or other things. The problem is not insurmountable, however, as is evidenced by the speed with which people learn how to operate remotely-controlled televisions and audio systems with keypads.

The most obvious implication for the classroom of poor keyboard skills is the slowness with which communication with the computer takes place. It is very frustrating to watch pupils search for letters on the keyboard, not just for the other pupils but for the teacher as well, and what could be an interesting exercise runs the risk of becoming a tediously slow and cumbersome one with predictable results: the class loses interest in the activity. It is not just speed of entry which I include under the heading of keyboard skills, however. Sometimes, the computer will wait for a response from the user, such as pushing an appropriate key before the computer moves on. At other times, it will be necessary to finish what one is typing by pressing the key marked 'return' or 'enter' before the computer will move on. In addition, there will be different ways of correcting mistakes in typing, depending upon the computer used. A general familiarity with computers is necessary before knowing all of these things and, even then, a period of familiarization is probably going to be necessary whenever one starts using a different type of computer for the first time.

It is not surprising, therefore, that one issue which is beginning to surface for general debate is whether or not we should teach keyboard skills, and if so at what age and, in secondary schools, in which subject area. I believe that the earlier a child becomes familiar with a keyboard the better: both for the pupil, because it will then become as natural to use a keyboard as a writing tool, and for the schools, because we will not then have to make a special provision for it. The best way, in my opinion, to develop keyboard skills is through usage, not through the normal 'transmission-of-skills' approach of subject-based curricula, because, if the reason for using the computer becomes important for the child early on, the motivation for becoming adept in its use is heightened. If we were to institute lessons in keyboard skills, it would be difficult to conceive of a rational context for them and the pupils would, perhaps, begin to see keyboard skills as yet another hoop through which teachers were intent on seeing them jump.

How, then, are we to overcome the problem? I feel that the first step is to develop a school-wide policy on computers, so that pupils come into contact with computers as often as possible over the course of their school careers. I do not mean that the pupils should spend every second of their school day typing, but, rather, that they see computers used in every part of the school and have the chance to use them whenever they form a natural part of their work. Pupils are not suddenly going to become fast typists, even if they spend several hours a week at a computer keyboard, so we should not imagine that the problem will be solved overnight. Instead, we must accept that, for some time to come, a factor in the use of the computer in the classroom will be the speed of typing, and make allowances for it. Of course, there are strategies which will help to minimize the impact on lessons, such as finding the quickest typist and using him or her when the whole class is working as a group with the computer or, when trying to make up small groups to work with the computer, make sure that each group has got at least one reasonable typist in it. In addition, teachers should make efforts to become reasonably proficient with computers, although the suggestion I have sometimes heard, of taking typing lessons, I consider to be rather extreme as it is not really necessary to be a touch-typist. The strategies suggested will not always be possible, of course, so perhaps one consideration to be taken into account when assessing software is how much typing is required and how the group will be able to cope with it.

Unfortunately, there is no easy answer to this problem of a lack of keyboard skills, but I am sure that it will become less important as time passes. In the meantime, it may be worth investigating alternative keyboards, especially for the younger pupils.

ALTERNATIVE KEYBOARDS

In the foregoing section, I was concerned with the problems connected with the conventional (QWERTY) keyboard layout which was adopted by all of the main computer producers. Whether it is true or not that the keyboard was designed the way it is so that it would slow typists down in order to make fewer mistakes, there is no doubt that it does pose problems for new users. It is no surprise, therefore, that a number of attempts have been made to design a keyboard which is simpler to use, without the strange arrangement of letters of QWERTY. Eventually it is entirely possible that keyboards will become obsolete as speech-recognition becomes more sophisticated (see page 66) and the most efficient method of communicating with the computer. The use of alternative keyboards is not widespread yet and there is some force in the argument, which was used with ITA, that it may be counter-productive to teach pupils to use one particular type of keyboard when eventually they will have to learn to use another. Nevertheless, these other types of keyboard are available and only time will tell how useful they are.

The first of these alternatives is called the Quinkey, an educational version of a Microwriter, a hand-held word processor. The design of these instruments is such that the hand fits neatly into a shaped surface: when the hand is in position, the fingertips are very close to five buttons and there is a sixth button at the side. A press on one button, or a combination of them, produces all the letters of the alphabet, numbers, symbols and features which appear on a normal typewriter. This may sound rather complicated, but it is surprisingly easy to learn these combinations. The Quinkey is attached to a computer by a cable, and up to four can be connected at the same time – a special program splits the screen into four, so that each user works on one quarter of the screen independently of the others and can edit, print and store text. There have been field trials, which were successful by all accounts – one teacher was extremely enthusiastic about it:

This project has dispelled the principles of 30 years of teaching. The Quinkey has helped the children reflect on what they are doing and it certainly gives them more confidence. Ideas like doing a school magazine are emerging. It's incredible! A whole new meaning has been given to writing.

(*Educational Computing*, June 1984, 11)

Having used one myself, albeit quite briefly, I can see how pupils would find the Quinkey far less daunting than the strange arrangement of letters on a normal keyboard. However, *Educational Computing*'s claim that the Quinkey gives you 'Four computers for the price of one' (ibid.) I find a little too extreme.

Next there is the Concept Keyboard, which is rather like a large board connected to the computer by a cable. It has a number of touch-sensitive pads on its surface and these can be programmed either singly or in blocks to provide areas which, when touched, cause a particular command to be executed by the computer. A simple overlay, with the commands printed on it, enables the user to see which areas produce the different commands. It seems to me that this would be an interesting way of introducing children to the computer at an early age, mainly, of course, because there is no need for the commands to be written in words, they could be pictograms or colours instead. The overlay can be written on with a soluble felt-tip pen in different colours to draw attention to particular commands and this would be very useful, for example, in teaching children the need to type 'return' after a command. This is, perhaps, the least complicated of the alternative keyboards, but it does not have the portability of the Quinkey.

Finally there is the 'Mouse' which has not yet filtered through to educational circles, although it appears that the new RML Nimbus is designed to incorporate its use. It was developed for business machines and consists of a small round object with a rolling ball underneath it, which is connected to the computer by a cable. The computer senses the movement of the Mouse and mirrors its movement on the screen with a white blob. On the screen will be either text or pictorial representations of objects corresponding to particular functions: for example, one major application of the Mouse is for a computer office where there are various facilities, such as document production, calculations of sales figures and information displayed as graphs or charts. Each function has a pictorial representation on the screen and, if the user wishes to select one, he moves the Mouse around on any flat surface until the white blob on the screen is over the right picture (called an 'icon'), then presses the Mouse down – the signal telling the computer that that is the function selected. I do not doubt that this principle will be adapted for most computers before long and it will thus become widely available for schools. Whether it does have possibilities for classroom use in any extensive way, I am not sure, because it cannot be used to enter text, unless the alphabet were printed and the Mouse used to build text letter by letter, but this would be rather cumbersome and probably not as quick as the QWERTY keyboard.

One unifying feature of all of these alternative keyboards is that they are attempting to circumvent the traditional keyboard, but they are all 'extras', whereas every computer is sold with a keyboard included in the price. As long as they face that sort of competition, they will only ever be an alternative, especially for education where cost is such an important factor. Nevertheless, the fact that they have been developed at all indicates that there will come a time when the QWERTY keyboard is a thing of the past.

Lesson preparation

An important aspect of all teaching, the preparation of lessons becomes vital when using the computer, because of the nature of the activities undertaken and the need for the teacher to be familiar with the program. A recent report (Horner, 1983) showed that lesson preparation frequently went haywire because of factors outside the control of teachers, such as room changes, alterations to timetable, staff absence or machine breakdown. Most teachers deal quite well with situations such as these more or less cheerfully, so using a computer need not necessarily increase the pressures on them in this respect. However, there are some new types of preparation with which teachers may not be so familiar.

The main item is, of course, becoming conversant with the program. There is a very good argument for software being examined by a complete department at the same time: this can help preparation in a number of ways. Firstly, all teachers in the department have the chance to see together how a program works, saving time with the computer – four people spending an hour looking at a program is more efficient than each individual spending a separate hour on the computer. This has the added benefit of increasing the confidence of those teachers who are less confident about using the computer, as well as being more in-service training. Secondly, the department as a whole can think collectively about how the program can be used in the classroom, sharing ideas for the benefit of the department as a whole – something which is never done enough in schools, no matter how often the sharing of ideas takes place. In sessions such as these, it is, perhaps, a good idea to work through the complete program from beginning to end, attempting not only to understand how the program works but also trying to make mistakes the children will make and seeing what happens. This last is very important, but is frequently overlooked by teachers – it is useful, to say the least, to know how the program copes with errors and how the teacher can avoid such errors happening. That is not to say that it would be a disaster for a teacher to be put into the position where the pupil asks for help and the teacher hasn't the faintest idea how to solve the problem: although this may be embarrassing if it happens very frequently, it puts both the teacher and the pupil in the same position and I have found that it is situations like these which have resulted in some very rewarding experiences as we try to solve a problem together – discovery learning for all concerned! It must, therefore, be accepted that no amount of 'playing' with the program before its use in the classroom will uncover all of the possible errors or difficult situations which might occur, but an understanding of the program as a whole is an important first step.

It may be during this departmental session that the question arises of how 'childproof' the program is. I mean by this that, with all computers, there is a way of interrupting the program while it is running, by pressing the 'Break' or 'Esc' keys on the BBC or the 'Ctrl' and 'Z' keys on the RML. Pupils do not take long to realize that this is possible, especially those who have computers at home, and some will take great delight in being able to 'break into' a program in this way. In some cases, this can be an advantage: for example, if it is possible to 'list' the program, that is, display the lines of the program itself, it will be possible to see how various calculations or procedures are carried out and they can then be modified to suit the group, although this does take an understanding of the programming language. On the other hand, interrupting the program can lose work in some circumstances, an annoying and often frustrating occurrence. In some cases, it is possible to prevent pupils from 'breaking into' programs, either by amending the program listing or by putting particular instructions on a computer disc. An example of the latter, a program called TURNKEY, is distributed with RML computers. When the computer is first switched on and the disc put into the drive, the system must be 'booted', that is, switched on, by pressing the letter 'B'. The computer then takes instructions from the disc about how it will load programs from the disc and a prompt appears on the screen. At this point, the user has to type in the name of the program he requires and it will be loaded. The program TURNKEY enables the user to make a disc 'self-booting', that is, all the user has to do after placing the disc in the drive is to type 'B' and the computer automatically loads the selected program and starts it running. This is quite useful, because, should the user attempt to get out of the program, the computer will reload the selected program and it will be very difficult for the user to list it. Although this is an over-simplified description, it does, I hope, show that it is possible, though not always desirable, to prevent pupils breaking into programs.

When it comes to the individual planning a lesson, or, more likely, a sequence of lessons using the computer, the type of activity involved will be determined by the program itself and the teacher's approach to it. First, the appropriate groupings must be chosen (see below) and then supporting material must be developed. The nature of the supporting material will depend upon the activities associated with the program, of course, but I find that one material which is invaluable is what is often referred to as an 'idiot sheet', although I take great pains to call it something else. This is a sheet which is left with the computer explaining how to operate the program and, where necessary, how to get out of difficult situations which might arise. This is a convenience for the teacher, because it does cut down on the number of times one is called to the computer to sort out the same problem for different groups, but it also encourages the pupils to use the computer independently of the teacher and thus feel in control of the situation. Often the materials provided will not be used and others will have to be developed in response to events in the classroom, but it is useful if there is a central bank of such materials and other resources where all teachers can see what has been used before and what has worked with others.

There are two main ways in which to incorporate the computer in lessons: either as one element amongst a number of others, or as a starting point. I have shown in Chapter 3 how various programs can be used for specific purposes within a series of lessons built around a class reader, the computer programs performing a particular function within a larger scheme of work. The programs themselves may well have other applications, or lend themselves to other types of work, but in this mode of use, their scope will be deliberately restricted. One problem about this approach is the familiarity of the pupils with particular programs: if it is going to take a long time for the pupils to learn how to use a program, even for restricted purposes, then this may well interrupt the scheme of work and the program might take on more significance for the pupils than the overall objective. If, for example, it will take a week for pupils to learn how to use the VIEWDATA program before they become suitably proficient at operating it, how viable is its use as only one element of many? It is clear, therefore, that it would be best to use programs with which the pupils are already familiar, or which will take only the minimum of time to introduce. An aspect of planning for using programs in this way is thus to introduce particular programs to the pupils *before* they are used within a scheme of work, which implies that planning should be long-term rather than short-term – another argument in favour of a departmental approach to computer use.

Using a computer program as the basis of a scheme of work presupposes not only that the program is flexible enough to be used in this manner, but also that the teacher is thoroughly familiar with it. Flexibility is often in the eye of the beholder, of course, and a program which some may see as having only one application will present a plethora of ideas to others: this boils down to the imagination of the teacher. There will always be, thank heavens, teachers whose vision and imagination enable them to realize the full potential of resources, but what of the rest of us? This is where contact between teachers can bring great benefits and why I would suggest that research into how other teachers are using particular programs should form a part of lesson preparation. The role of advisory staff and other bodies is crucial here, for how are teachers to know what other teachers are doing when we have, in the past, been isolated? Support services for classroom teachers are vital if we are to take full advantage of the potential of the computer.

One approach to planning work based around a program was shown to me by Jean Melton, a teacher of 9- and 10-year-olds at Olney Middle School in Buckinghamshire. She had obtained a program called SPACEX, an adventure game requiring the user to collect various parts of a spaceship which have been hidden on the planet Persephone by its inhabitants, the Kleptoes. From playing with the program herself, she developed the diagram in Figure 6. The program itself, although at the centre of the diagram, is only central to the scheme of work in that it is a starting point, a common experience which the children can utilize in the activities surrounding it, the true focus of the diagram. Developing such a 'map' can be a very useful method of evaluating a program's potential, regardless of how it is to be used in the classroom.

Whilst these considerations will be more or less the same in all schools, the amount of time to be spent with the computer will differ from school to school and from middle to secondary schools. I have virtually always underestimated the amount of time it will take to get through the work associated with one program and I know, from conversations with other teachers, that this is a common experience. In a middle school, where teachers sometimes stay with their class for large parts of the day, this may not be so much of a problem, with the possibility of extending the time spent on one activity, whereas those in secondary schools will have to face the problem of a rigid timetable which cannot be altered for one activity. In these circumstances, it will be necessary to break the activities up into sections which will not only fit into the allotted time spans, but will also provide some continuity for the pupils, something not always possible. I have found that it is quite useful to have a 'reporting-back' session towards the end of each lesson and that this encourages the taking of notes about the activities, provides an exchange of experiences and provides a natural assessment of the activities which have been taking place during the lesson. At the beginning of the following lesson, a quick résumé by me soon reminds the groups how far they have got, especially when they refer to their notes on the previous lesson.

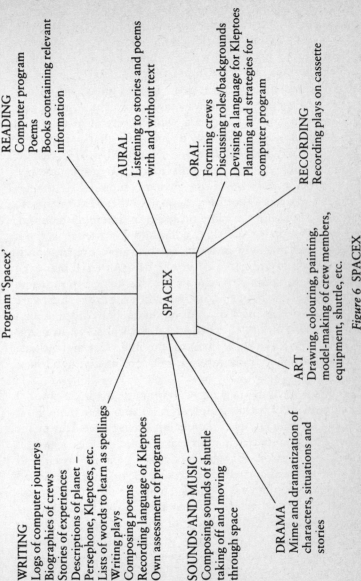

COMPUTER SKILLS
Program 'Spacex'

READING
Computer program
Poems
Books containing relevant
information

AURAL
Listening to stories and poems
with and without text

ORAL
Forming crews
Discussing roles/backgrounds
Devising a language for Kleptoes
Planning and strategies for
computer program

RECORDING
Recording plays on cassette

ART
Drawing, colouring, painting,
model-making of crew members,
equipment, shuttle, etc.

DRAMA
Mime and dramatization of
characters, situations and
stories

SOUNDS AND MUSIC
Composing sounds of shuttle
taking off and moving
through space

WRITING
Logs of computer journeys
Biographies of crews
Stories of experiences
Descriptions of planet –
Persephone, Kleptoes, etc.
Lists of words to learn as spellings
Writing plays
Composing poems
Recording language of Kleptoes
Own assessment of program

SPACEX

Figure 6 SPACEX

Another possibility for those with rigid timetable restrictions is to seek the support and participation of another department. It does seem to me that the computer offers an excellent opportunity to break down the subject barriers and allow pupils to get away from the impression that English is important only in room 24, or that geography is important only in room 22. Many programs now available have the attribute that they demand from the pupils a wide variety of abilities and knowledge and very rarely can one state that a particular program is only applicable to one subject. MARY ROSE, for example, demands language skills, maths, geography and history, to name only the most obvious 'subjects'. If time is restricted, it seems a good idea to involve other departments, so that pupils will use the same program in different areas and, hopefully, begin to see that skills and knowledge are not compartmentalized. In order to do this, more preparation is needed, for a co-ordinated effort will be required. It may even be possible in secondary schools for the summer term to be earmarked for work of such a kind, when the exam classes are over, exam papers marked, and that marvellous air of relaxation can be felt around the corridors! It is surprising how useful such an exercise can be, both for the pupils and for the teachers, who will probably only rarely experience at first hand how other departments work.

For those who have never used a computer in the classroom I have one word of warning, however: no amount of planning is going to prevent a disaster happening at least once. During his or her career, every teacher has experienced the disintegration of a planned lesson, for whatever reason, and in virtually all cases the teacher has carried on, having learnt from it. It is a sad thing that one disaster with a computer can make some teachers reject it completely. Often, the cause of the problem is not the computer itself, but a poor choice of program, or an unsuitable approach which has resulted in the bad lesson. More than with any other teaching aid, teachers must go back to being learners, which is no bad thing, and must realize that what we tell our pupils – 'Keep trying, David, you'll get it right eventually' – is true just as much for us as for them.

Organization of pupils

I have often heard the complaint from teachers that they have only one computer and thirty-plus pupils, implying that there is really very little they can do in that situation. Whilst it is true that with traditional resources – say, books – one between thirty would seem unworkable, the same cannot be said of a computer which is so much more flexible. It would be strange, for example, for teachers to argue that each pupil needed a complete school library to himself, yet, in a sense, the principle is the same. The chief problem is, of course, *access* to resources: whilst a library will provide each pupil with access to a number of books each, one computer to thirty pupils appears to offer only limited access on an individual basis. Yet, using the illustration of the library, would any teacher set pupils a task which meant that all the pupils had to use just one book? Of course not: the teacher would ensure that the tasks were varied enough so that there would not be an overwhelming demand for a small number of books. With a computer the idea is the same – if there is only one available, it must be used efficiently and in such a way that not all the pupils will need to use it at once. In fact, I find the idea of each pupil sitting in front of his own computer quite frightening: it brings closer a situation where computers would inhibit communication rather than facilitate it. The solution to the problem (if problem it is) of one computer and a large number of pupils lies, therefore, in, firstly, the structuring of activities to use the computer efficiently and, secondly, the organizing of pupils to provide appropriate access to it. The first solution will be covered in the preparation of lessons (see page 119), where the choice of which activities to use will be determined by the number of computers available and the number of pupils involved. The second solution, however, needs further consideration.

There are three main types of organizing possible: whole-group, small-group and individual. It should not be thought, however, that it is impossible to mix them, for varying groupings within a lesson not only gives a range of working environments, but also provides variety, especially with less able pupils whose concentration spans may be quite limited.

i) Whole group

This organization will probably be the starting point for most programs, because it is generally a good idea to demonstrate the program before it is used by the pupils, so that they can see what the program does. With programs such as adventure games, one has to be quite careful how much is shown. It is also, for the teacher, a 'gentle' introduction to the use of the computer, because it provides a fair degree of control over events.

This organization does have severe limitations, however. One of the most interesting aspects of using the computer in the classroom for me has been the way pupils use the same program in different ways and, of course, one of the benefits of the computer is that it will encourage a wide range of discussion, but in order for these things to happen the pupils must be involved in the process. When the computer is being used with a whole group, that involvement is threatened and the drawbacks of whole-group discussions apply with equal force. There are a few programs which can be used successfully in this way – the program TRAY, for example (see page 52) – but the majority are inappropriate for use in this way. This type of grouping should be used sparingly, therefore.

ii) Small group

This grouping is the most suitable whenever the computer is being used in the classroom, regardless of how many computers are available. Working in small groups not only involves all of the pupils in the work but also increases the interaction between them, an activity long regarded as being of great value (see, for example, The Bullock Report). It has the added advantage of freeing the teacher from part of the management of the activity and allows him to become a partner in the lesson. Three or four pupils appears to be the optimum number for the groups: any more than that and the possibility of some not being involved in the activity increases.

Of course, this does demand more of the teacher than whole-group work, because the groups not using the computer will need work prepared which is related to the program being used, materials which the teacher, more often than not, will have to develop by himself or herself. In addition, as was noted earlier, the teacher can feel a sense of insecurity when the computer takes over part of his or her management role. In the early stages of computer use, I felt a tremendous urge to be near the computer all of the time, partly because if anything 'went wrong' I would be on the spot, and partly because I wanted to see what was happening. It takes a fair degree of self-control to keep away, but this is necessary as there is nothing like the presence of the teacher to inhibit group interaction.

iii) Individual use

Although this may seem a very inappropriate form of organization, particularly when there is only one computer available, there are occasions when it can be useful. The advantages of this mode of use centre upon the contact with the program which one user will have on his own: for example, pupils with learning difficulties or a handicap. Nevertheless, it is possible to envisage other circumstances when a single pupil could use the computer – perhaps contributing to a story, written on a word-processor, which is built up by individuals in turn. In this case, one pupil could be writing while others are engaged on another activity.

The drawbacks to this are obvious, however. There is the danger that the other pupils will not only be jealous of the pupil using the computer, but also they may be far more interested in what he is doing than what they should be doing. Then, the program would have to be foolproof so that the teacher would not be called to leave the rest of the group in order to deal with a problem. Finally, the isolation of the individual would also rob him of any interaction while using the computer.

Purely from a consideration of the possible groupings, therefore, it can be seen that using a computer in the classroom makes different demands on the teacher when compared with traditional teaching techniques, and these must be learnt through experience. I believe that using one computer with a group is, in many respects, the best way of coming to terms with the technology and the necessary teaching practices, which is why I feel that no matter how many computers are available within a school, starting with one is a good idea. I am sure that one of the reasons why many language laboratories are lying idle or have been dismantled is that, although they have a great deal of potential in the teaching of languages, they require a set of teaching and technical skills which teachers did not have the time to acquire. We run similar risks if we assume that using a computer is no different from 'ordinary' teaching and it would be waste on a massive scale – not just in economic terms – if school computers suffered the same fate as that of language laboratories. Of course, once a teacher has experience of using one computer in a classroom, the expertise he has developed will stand him in good stead for using more than one: in a sense, we must learn to walk before we attempt to run.

Evaluation

One of the ways in which a teacher will gain expertise with the computer is through evaluation of its use in his or her lessons. Most experienced teachers know instinctively how a particular lesson has gone, but where the computer is an innovation the evaluative process does need to be a little more formal. Initially, therefore, I would suggest that there are three main areas for consideration. Firstly, there are the practical aspects. Under this heading, I would include the groupings selected, not only in terms of whether the most appropriate organization was chosen, but also whether the composition of the groups created any problems. I have found that sometimes, when I have allowed the pupils to select their own groups, one group has contained 'computer freaks' and the others none at all, which means that the other groups may well struggle with the technology rather than the task in hand. This is particularly true in the early stages of computer use, so I would recommend that any such 'computer freaks' should be well distributed around the groups because their confidence with the computer very quickly 'rubs off' on the others and speeds up both the process of familiarization and the progress of the group with relation to keyboard skills. Another practical aspect worthy of evaluation is the physical arrangement of the classroom, which can throw up unforeseen problems, no matter how much preparation and thought have gone into it before the lesson.

Secondly, there is the program itself, an evaluation of which will not only benefit the teacher who has used it, but also others in the department or school who may wish to use it. This is, of course, distinct from the initial evaluation of the program when it first arrived in the school. It may be that 'bugs' are discovered and ways must be found to either avoid or cure them; or that there is a line of work that develops from the program which became clear only when it was being used. Even if the program fulfils expectations, it is worth evaluating the reasons for its success, so that this can be borne in mind for future purchases.

Thirdly, the supporting material and resulting work should be evaluated. It may be that the approach to the program or its associated work needs to be changed in some way, in order to cope with the unexpected or to bring out aspects of the program which were not covered in the original planning. Any written work can, of course, give a good guide to whether the program achieved the objectives set for it and how deeply, or otherwise, the pupils were involved in the activity. Evaluating the talk that went on is a little more difficult, because, in all probability, the teacher did not listen to each group. In the end, one can only assess what one heard, although questioning each group about what they have done can give a good indication of what was or was not discussed by them.

I have stressed the need for the individual teacher to evaluate the use of the computer, but this need not be a solitary activity. It is useful to ask the pupils themselves whether they found the work valuable or not. Sometimes they are aware of aspects of lessons when the computer is being used which the teacher is not and they can make valuable suggestions about the use of the program in the future. Another very useful input can be obtained from colleagues observing the lesson, because, especially in the early stages of computer use, it is often the case that they will notice things which the teacher is too busy or preoccupied to hear or see. It can have another benefit: after having seen me use the computer with one group, a self-confessed 'technophobe' went away determined to use the computer with her groups. I am sure that many teachers who do not yet use the computer in their teaching would start to do so if they saw another teacher using it successfully.

I believe that evaluation is just as important as preparation, if not more so, for it paves the way to future success, not only for the teacher and his department but also for the pupils. Further, the results of the evaluative process are, I feel, too important in this new and fast-developing field to be kept within a school: the authors of a particular program would more than welcome such feedback as a way of improving the program and developing new ones and other teachers would find the lessons learnt a very useful aid in their own teaching. Reviews of programs and details of how they have been used (successfully or otherwise) should be freely available, but, in practice, they are not. I have listed in the Reference Section the addresses of two journals which do publish such reviews, but this is another area where local advisory staff could provide a useful service to their teachers – by circulating an annotated list of programs being used in their area and the schools using them, so that others can make contact.

CONCLUSIONS

In this chapter, I have tried to indicate some of the ways in which using a computer as a teaching aid places new demands on teachers and some of the consequent implications for classroom practice. I hope that it is now evident that, far from being a replacement for the teacher, it is only the teacher's presence and skill which can possibly channel the computer's flexibility and power into the creation of exciting learning experiences. There is no doubt in my mind that computers and computer-related technology will transform the face of education, but the burden of that transformation will fall upon the already hard-pressed classroom teacher: it is he or she, after all, who will have to develop the new skills, something which will consume a great deal of that rarest of commodities – time. The responsibility is great, therefore, upon those whose job it is to support teachers to provide them with the wherewithal to develop the new skills, to examine the implications of the new technology and to keep abreast of new developments. In the end, of course, this will depend upon central government's willingness to fund such things as in-service training, the support services themselves and research into various aspects of the use of the computer in education. Let us hope that their determination to see a computer in every school will be matched by a determination to see them being used effectively.

7

THEORY INTO PRACTICE

No theory is good except on condition that
one use it to go beyond.
(Gide, *Journals*)

In order to 'bring into focus' some of the practical suggestions I
have made elsewhere in this book, I would like to include two
case studies so that the translation of these suggestions into
schemes of work and lessons can be more easily understood.
These case studies should be seen as anecdotes rather than
studious classroom research. Their purpose is not to prescribe
but, rather, to show that one does not have to be anything other
than a teacher to use the computer in the classroom: the
techniques and considerations may be different from the
more 'traditional' approach, but they are soon learnt through
experience.

Case study 1

School: A rural secondary modern school with approximately 600 pupils who come from surrounding
villages. Approximately 27 per cent of the pupils
either have their own home computers or have
had experience with computers at feeder
schools.

Program: TRAY
Class: Twenty-seven first-year pupils (12-year-olds) of mixed ability who have no previous experience of using the computer in English.
Lessons: Two per week, Tuesday and Friday: both lasting one hour and five minutes.

SCHEME OF WORK

The half-term's work was to be built around a class reader, *Last Stand at Goodbye Gulch* by Rex Benedict. This was the first book we were going to work on in any detail and I wanted a variety of approaches in order to overcome the resistance other classes had shown to what has become a less popular genre in recent years.

Week 1:   Introduction to the genre: discussion of conventions, historical details. Compilation of a list of words associated with Westerns, names of characters (invented or real) and descriptive details.

Week 2:   Introduction of TRAY: two texts – one written by me, containing many of the words discussed during the previous week, one to be taken from the book.

Week 3:   Begin reading the book: start with me reading, then volunteers. Some private reading with follow-up questions to vary approach. Discussion of events, characters.

Week 4:   Continue reading: pupils start writing short passages in the style and vocabulary of the genre.

Week 5:   Continue reading: hear one or two of the pupils' pieces of writing.

Week 6:   Finish reading the book. Split into seven groups: several activities: (*i*) working with TRAY, (*ii*) making 'Wanted' posters, (*iii*) making newspapers around the incidents in the book, (*iv*) drawing maps of the area in the book.

Week 7: Finish work, 'round off'.

Week 1

The first week's lessons were 'standard' lessons, with class discussion involving only the most vociferous pupils, but most of the work was covered. It was surprising how few of the pupils had any more than a passing knowledge of the genre, so I quickly introduced two extracts from *Spoil the Child* by Howard Fast, which was received quite well. From this, I asked the pupils to start drawing up their own list of words and phrases with the idea that it would be useful when writing their own stories – I did not mention the computer at all.

Their lists were fairly predictable, although some of the names were quite inventive – 'Gun 'em down Daniels' and 'Sheriff Killer Kennedy'. Many of the names were of other pupils in the group, so there was some element of parody.

Historical details were sparse, so I set some research for homework. This was not very successful. I therefore gave them some background information and promised to return to this aspect later if there was any interest (there wasn't!).

Week 2

Lesson 1

I managed to set up the computer before they arrived in the room – no easy undertaking – so there was a great deal of interest as they entered. I had to gently deflect those 'computer freaks' among them who were continually asking questions about the computer, but it took a while to get them settled. I introduced the purpose of the lesson briefly because I could see that some were extremely eager to get started with the computer.

Initially, there was too much attention on the computer and what it was displaying on the screen, rather than on the activity itself, but, as the program is presented as a game, I was able to divert their attention by referring repeatedly to the score. I had decided to operate the computer myself, as the novelty element would disappear very quickly if the keyboarding was too slow, so I was able to get straight into the activity rather than spending time explaining to a new operator which keys to press.

Within a short space of time, all of them were deeply involved in the activity, which was to uncover the following passage, written by me, which contains a number of words included in their lists:

> *It was sunrise. The doors of the saloon were swinging gently in the breeze which brought tumbleweed into the town every day. At one end of the street Sureshot Pete appeared, his six-guns at the ready. The Sheriff of Wing City strode out of his office, ready to face the showdown.*
>
> *Pete drew first and loosed off two quick shots, but the Sheriff's aim was truer and Pete fell to the floor fatally wounded.*
>
> *'Bury me on Boot Hill,' he groaned.*
> *'Sure thing, Pete,' the Sheriff replied, smiling.*

Two words in particular bothered me a little, 'tumbleweed' and 'truer', but I was interested to see how successful the children would be with them.

After the initial success with the more obvious one- and two-letter words, they began to grind to a halt, so I introduced the idea of 'buying' letters and there followed a brief discussion about which was the most useful letter to buy. Subsequent use of this program has taught me that a new group will nearly always choose vowels, which is not necessarily the best choice, but I forced back the temptation to influence their decision.

As the lesson progressed, their enthusiasm did not dwindle and they were getting on very well indeed. Every child had made some suggestion and I was aware that all were riveted by the activity. Unfortunately, in winding up the lesson I forgot to 'save' the incomplete text, which meant that we had to begin again in the next lesson.

Lesson 2

I didn't have time to set the computer up before they arrived, so the first ten minutes of the lesson were lost, but, while I was putting it all together, they started adding to their lists. When I was ready, I told them that we had to start from scratch, which was greeted with some dismay, and I was anticipating that I would have to help in order to quickly reach the point at which we had left the exercise.

I was surprised to find that many could repeat, almost word-for-word, large parts of the text we had uncovered in the previous lesson, so we were soon at the point where we had left off. Some had even been considering blanks which looked particularly difficult – they were determined to achieve a high score, so did not wish to buy letters, except as a last resort. There were a few parts which proved more difficult than I had anticipated: 'groaned', 'fatally' and, as expected, 'truer'. 'Tumbleweed' was uncovered very quickly: they had bought the 'e's in the last lesson and someone had done some thinking, which gave them 'eweed' and it was not long before the rest was decoded.

There was just as much enthusiasm for most of the rest of the lesson, but, towards the end, a couple of children were beginning to 'wander' a little. I made a point of asking them for their suggestions, and the others' fascination for completing the text helped to ease the problem.

The cheer which greeted the final uncovering was probably heard at the other end of the school, so I was in no doubt about their sense of achievement. Some immediately asked for another text (which I had planned), but I was aware of some loss of interest, so we immediately started reading the book itself, and I was able to draw their attention to the language used and the way that the story starts, by relating it to the text uncovered. Although this only occupied the last ten minutes or so, the discussion involved many more pupils than previously.

I had not introduced them to the operation of the program, knowing that it was going to be a number of weeks before they would have to use it, and I had no doubt that they would remember the overall appearance of the screen, so would need little reminding. During both lessons, I had arranged the computer so that the monitor was facing me and a large TV facing the group. This meant that they did not have to move at all and provided a fairly rigid structure for what could have been a very unstructured situation: their attention was easily focused, because, in a sense, it was almost like a blackboard lesson in terms of physical layout.

Weeks 3, 4 and 5

The reading of the book was accomplished without anything notable happening. Their reactions to it were mixed, although all liked at least one of the characters – they are quite quirky and well-defined in the book. I interspersed the reading with work on a short passage by them in the style and vocabulary of the genre, having told them that they would have to provide one passage for another group to uncover using TRAY. This led to discussion about what constituted a 'difficult' word, whether there were certain letter combinations which were unusual or potentially misleading and so on.

By the fifth week, we had all but finished the book and most of the pupils had completed a short piece of writing. We listened to two pieces and tried to decide whether they would be difficult to uncover in TRAY. I took in both for later use with the computer.

Week 6

Lesson 1

We finished reading the book and spent some time discussing it. The book as a whole was voted a qualified hit, but the character Grunt had friends in every quarter.

I then set up the groups and activities, allowing the pupils a free choice, with a maximum of four per group. There was tremendous interest and expectation about using the computer, although one group was clearly hesitant about being able to operate it. I chose that group to go on the computer first because there was a possibility that the members would need quite a lot of help (as it turned out, they didn't), but they had some work to do before they could start using it.

While I was setting up the computer, all the groups began by drawing a map of the area described in the book, except the group which I had decided would use the computer first which began putting together a short piece of text. I had put a limit of ten sentences on each piece of text to make it possible for each group to have a go in the time available. By the end of the lesson, the first group had completed its task, and some of the other groups had started on the newspaper articles.

Lesson 2

I provided the first group with a piece of text to uncover and 'let them loose' on it, having left an 'idiot sheet' clearly visible. Fortunately, the program is simple to operate, so, after a few minutes, this group needed no further help. I set a time limit of fifteen minutes on uncovering the text and went around the other groups to see what they were doing.

The first group of pupils finished within the time limit, and were very pleased with themselves because they had only had to 'buy' three letters, and their score was, apparently, very high, although by no means the best of all the groups, eventually. I then spent a couple of minutes typing in their piece of text for the next group (I can type reasonably quickly: in subsequent use, when there was more time available, I had decided

I would let the pupils do this). The next group came on, having finished writing their piece of text.

Needless to say, it was all fairly chaotic, but the groups on the computer needed very little help, so I could concentrate on the others. There was a great deal of interest in what the group on the computer was doing, and there was a rush to sharpen pencils at the front from where they could see what was happening on the monitor. Nevertheless, we did manage to get a lot done, and by the end of the lesson three groups had used the computer. I collected in the pieces of text from those groups who had not yet used the computer, so that I could type them in over the weekend.

Week 7

Lesson 1

Once again, I had managed to set the computer up before the group arrived, so we were able to 'get into the swing of things' very quickly. I had anticipated that the lesson would be very busy, because there were four groups to use the computer, and, once they had all arrived and settled, just under an hour in which to do it.

More by luck than anything else, all of the groups managed to use the computer by the end of the lesson – helped by one group which uncovered its text in double-quick time. Not all of the groups finished the complete text, but we noted scores and formed a league table to decide the 'winners'. I had thought quite hard about this, because I did not wish to encourage blind guesswork, but, in the event, the pressure of time and of achieving as high a score as possible did work to advantage, so that what I did overhear and see around the computer was almost entirely task-oriented and extremely purposeful!

All of the groups had done most of the other tasks set, but there was some finishing off to do. By and large, the rest of the work was done well and the enthusiasm generated by the computer 'washed over' into the other activities.

Lesson 2

We spent the first part of the lesson 'finishing off' all of the set tasks, but I did want to use the computer once more. I had typed in the first few sentences of the book and presented it as a TRAY text for uncovering. This was meant as much for relaxation as for a serious task and my pupils took to it with gusto, armed with their newly acquired expertise. It took them a matter of minutes to recognize the text and we spent the rest of the lesson discussing what clues there were that had led them to spot it, ending up with each pupil saying in one sentence what he thought of the book as a whole.

EVALUATION

Overall, the scheme of work was a success, more than I could have anticipated. There is little doubt that the computer added extra interest for the pupils, especially as it was the first time I had used it with this class. They enjoyed the variety of approach and seemed to respond well to the group work during the last two weeks. How much the computer contributed is difficult to assess accurately. With regard to their writing and general appreciation of the more technical aspects of language, it did have some impact, as they took part in discussions which contained a great deal of reference to these things, mostly initiated by themselves. Of course, there is no panacea, so any lessons learnt will need further revision, but it is comforting to know that, in future, when I wish to draw attention to some grammatical point, I can either refer to or use this program. The biggest impact the computer had on this class, remembering that they had no experience of the computer in English before this, was the general level of enthusiasm and animation it introduced, which made it a great deal easier to work with the class.

In retrospect, I did try to cram too much into a short space of time, although the time element in uncovering the texts worked well. Another class I tried this with were not so successful at completing the texts in the time allowed and were rather frustrated by the whole experience. On the other hand, both classes took part enthusiastically in discussions about grammar and syntax in relation to the texts they were uncovering, something I would find great difficulty in approaching meaningfully in other situations.

In terms of organization, I had used the computer before this so I knew that the classroom-layout and group-work arrangements would work, although it was proved to me yet again that it is best to have the computer set up before the pupils arrive in the classroom: desirable but not always possible, so it is a very good idea to have something for them to do while the computer is being set up.

The program itself worked very well, and not once was I called on to deal with a technical problem. The 'idiot sheet' was simple to compile and provided the pupils with all they needed to know. Fortunately, none of them yet knew how to 'break out' of the program with this computer, so there were none of the associated problems.

Case study 2

School: A rural middle school with approximately 250 pupils who live either in the village or in others nearby. This school feeds a large comprehensive and, for those who pass an entrance examination, two grammar schools in a nearby town. Most pupils have had some experience of computers, either in leisure time or during lessons, although this has been relatively limited.

Program: MALLORY (MEP Primary Language Pack)

Class: Thirty-five 11–12-year-olds (fourth year middle school) of mixed ability who had used the computer before.

Lessons: One each day of roughly one hour's duration, for three weeks.

SCHEME OF WORK

Towards the end of a term, I wanted to revise, consolidate and build on work which had been done during the term. A different approach to those previously adopted was required, so I opted for group work using the computer. I wanted to use an adventure game or simulation, because my pupils had not used such a program with me before and I was aware that a number of them enjoyed adventure games either with their own computers or with the school computer in lunch hours. The game had to be one which did not take too long to solve or my class of thirty-five would not all be able to have a turn on the computer.

I chose MALLORY because I knew that it could be altered to suit the needs of the teacher/group. The program is an adventure game built around the idea of things having been stolen and the user takes the role of a policeman investigating the theft and moving around a large house questioning suspects and (hopefully) arresting the culprit. I decided to change the name of the program to 'Olney School', where the theft would take place. The suspects became members of the school staff, including the school secretary and caretaker. The items to be stolen ranged from the Headmaster's caravan to fifty maths books or a box of compasses. I altered the program so that each suspect would say something in keeping with their character: for example, the PE teacher, a season ticket holder of a well-known local club said, 'Watford supporters don't steal.'

I planned my work using the diagram in Figure 7 to identify the possible areas of work which could arise out of the program. Each group would be presented with a set of worksheets divided into two parts: (*i*) investigative work using the computer and (*ii*) individual and team work. The first part was to be used during and after the use of the computer, the second part was to be done while waiting to use the program and after completing the first part. As I was teaching a very mixed ability English group, I had to ensure that there was something for everybody.

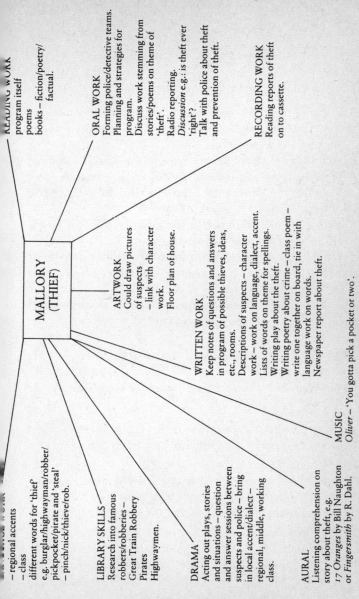

READING WORK
program itself
poems
books – fiction/poetry/
factual.

ORAL WORK
Forming police/detective teams.
Planning and strategies for
program.
Discuss work stemming from
stories/poems on theme of
'theft'.
Radio reporting.
Discussion e.g.: is theft ever
'right'?
Talk with police about theft
and prevention of theft.

RECORDING WORK
Reading reports of theft
on to cassette.

ARTWORK
Could draw pictures
of suspects
– link with character
work.
Floor plan of house.

WRITTEN WORK
Keep notes of questions and answers
in program of possible thieves, ideas,
etc., rooms.
Descriptions of suspects – character
work – work on language, dialect, accent.
Lists of words on theme for spellings.
Writing play about the theft.
Writing poetry about crime – class poem –
write one together on board, tie in with
language work on words.
Newspaper report about theft.

MALLORY
(THIEF)

MUSIC
Oliver – 'You gotta pick a pocket or two'.

– regional accents
– class
different words for 'thief'
e.g. burglar/highwayman/robber/
pickpocket/pirate and 'steal'
– pinch/nick/thieve/rob.

LIBRARY SKILLS
Research into famous
robbers/robberies –
Great Train Robbery
Pirates
Highwaymen.

DRAMA
Acting out plays, stories
and situations – question
and answer sessions between
suspects and police – bring
in local accent/dialect –
regional, middle, working
class.

AURAL
Listening comprehension on
story about theft, e.g.
17 *Oranges* by Bill Naughton
or *Fingersmith* by R. Dahl.

Figure 7 MALLORY

OLNEY SCHOOL

Investigative work using program

First Worksheet – using the computer

1 *Report* – Keep notes of what each suspect says in order to write a thorough report of the investigation for your superiors.
2 *Floor plan* – Draw a floor plan of the school, labelling both the rooms and where each of the suspects are.
3 *Stolen item* – Draw a picture and write a full description of the missing item giving its value.
4 *Suspects* – Sketch in pencil and describe fully the physical appearance of each of the suspects.
5 *Newspaper report* – Each member of the group must write a front-page report of the theft for a different local or national newspaper.
6 *Radio report* – The class must write a brief radio report of the theft and tape it on cassette.

Individual and team work

Second Worksheet – work away from the computer

1 *Interview*
Draw up a list of questions to ask a real policeman about different types of theft and how to prevent them.

2 *Newspaper cuttings*
Read local and national newspapers and cut out and mount reports about theft. Make clear in which newspaper the report appeared and the date when the story appeared.

3 *Thesaurus*
   i) How many different words for 'thief' can your team think of? Make a list of your words together with their dictionary definitions.

ii) How many different verbs can your team think of which mean 'to steal' in one way or another? Make a list of your words together with their dictionary definitions.

4 *Research*

Using the school library and/or any other source of information, each member of your group must research and write about one of the following:

i)	Dick Turpin	*vi*)	Sir Francis Drake
ii)	Robin Hood	*vii*)	Bonnie and Clyde
iii)	Ned Kelly	*viii*)	The Great Train Robbery
iv)	Blackbeard	*ix*)	Butch Cassidy and the
v)	Billy the Kid		Sundance Kid

5 *Story*

Each member of your group must write a story about a theft. It can be set in any time and can be about something as simple as a mugging or as complicated as a well-planned robbery.

6 *Cartoon*

Write and draw a cartoon strip with one of the following titles or make up a title of your own.

i) FICKO THE FIETH
ii) BILLY THE KID STRIKES AGAIN
iii) BRAINY THE BURGLAR
iv) DICK TURPIN RIDES ONCE MORE
v) CLARENCE THE CROOK AND HIS CRONIES

7 *Poem*

Write a poem about a theft or a thief.

8 *Play*

Your group must write a play about a theft of some sort. You may have to join forces with another group to act it out.

9 *Fiction*

Make a list of library books about a robbery or theft of some kind, together with a sentence or two about each book if possible.

COMMENTARY

I introduced the scheme of work by reading Roald Dahl's *The Hitch-hiker*. The class enjoyed it immensely and we discussed the characters and the dubious moral of the tale at length. I then told them that in their next English lesson they would be doing work in groups, some of which would be with the computer, and asked them to quickly choose with whom they wanted to work, in groups of three or four.

At the start of the next lesson, I went through the worksheets with the groups: some of the tasks were deliberately vague, so that I could spend some time with each group discussing what they were going to be doing. The biggest organizational problem was, of course, keeping the contents of the program secret, because, although the culprit is chosen randomly by the computer with each game, I didn't want to let the groups know in advance that the theft was based in our school, nor what each suspect said, as this remains constant. This was solved by placing the computer in the library, just down the corridor from my room, so that each group could use the computer out of the classroom. I had few worries about the children being in another room for a number of reasons: firstly, I had known most of them for two years and had built up a good relationship with them; secondly, there was a great deal of enthusiasm about using the computer and, finally, the novelty of the program itself was very likely to keep each group involved in the desired activity.

I deliberately chose a very able group to use the computer first, so that I could remain with the rest of the class. I directed them all to start with 'Interview' because I had invited a policeman to talk to the class that week, and each group had to think up ten sensible questions to ask. After they had done this, they could tackle the rest of the tasks in any order.

Once the class were settled into this, I went to the library where the first group were well into the program: they were getting on very well. One was using the keyboard, one was making notes on what each suspect said and the other was occupied with drawing a floor plan. They were delighted to see me and I was met with: 'Guess where you were? In the swimming pool! We found the stolen item in the Headmaster's study. It was his caravan. How could anyone get it in his study?'

Each group was sworn to secrecy so that the other groups could be surprised with the program. Once the research work got under way, and other groups were using the library, I had to 'hide' the group using the computer away from prying eyes. On reflection, I could have done this (just!) in the classroom, but, in the event, putting the computer in another room added a sense of mystery entirely in keeping with the idea of the program and ensured that the first few lessons set a pattern of work which allowed the groups not on the computer to concentrate on what they were doing.

Over the course of the next fortnight, the rest of the groups worked through the program and were deeply involved in completing the set tasks. I spent most of my time visiting the groups, encouraging where necessary, helping them to solve problems when they were encountered and, at the same time, assessing what the pupils were doing. As always, with work of this kind, finishing off can be very 'patchy', with some pupils having completed all the tasks and others still doing them. Each group's work was to be put in a folder for display in the school, so as each group finished I was able to set additional work such as designing a front cover for their folder, compiling a list of contents and providing extra illustrations. When there were only one or two left still completing the tasks, I asked the rest of the class to complete a questionnaire which asked them for their evaluation of the work they had been doing.

EVALUATION

The scheme worked well, and the computer program, although it depended upon novelty value to a large extent, nevertheless helped to generate a great deal of enthusiasm and motivation.

This is shown by the fact that each group spent at least part of the time working in the library, away from the classroom, yet did not take advantage of my absence.

In terms of the work connected with the computer part of the worksheets, I was very pleased with what the groups had done: it clearly demonstrated the fact that they had enjoyed the series of lessons and that my overall aim of consolidating work done previously had been achieved. There were weaker parts – the report, for example. In completing the report of their investigations, some groups very long-windedly wrote everything down word-for-word and only one group went so far as to tabulate what they had discovered. Another weakness was that some pupils did not understand that the Olney School in the program was not the real school, and that the connections between the locations in the program bore little relation to reality, except by accident. This led to some very strange floor plans being drawn.

On the other hand, some work turned out to be much better than I had anticipated. Only one newspaper report was required, but a number of groups wanted to write two: one about the crime itself and another about the capture of the thief. In fact, I developed this further and asked them to write a letter from the imprisoned thief to his or her family, which produced some amusing and thoughtful work. A great favourite was the radio report, which really captured their imaginations. One very slow learner asked if he could take the tape home with him over a weekend: by the Monday, he'd taped the 'News At Ten' theme and had written and read an excellent report. The task involving a sketch of the suspects surprised the pupils because they suddenly realized that they didn't look at people very closely.

The biggest problem I faced was in preventing some groups from becoming frustrated while waiting for their turn on the computer, especially the less able groups. It took over a week for all of them to use it, and the sense of mystery surrounding the program heightened their eagerness to begin. I overcame this by guiding them towards those activities I knew would probably interest them, such as the cartoons, and ensuring that the least able took their turn at the computer as soon as possible. As the least able needed a fair amount of time and help to discover the culprit, the other groups had to wait longer, but it was not difficult to steer them towards tasks which captured their interest.

With a group of thirty-five in one classroom there are always problems connected with space, and this series of lessons was no exception. Being able to place the computer in the library was a godsend in this respect, as it did create a little more room in which the other groups could work. Nevertheless, when it came to using the tape recorder, it was difficult to find a quiet spot for work. There is no real solution to this, at present.

The scheme of work did take a little longer to get through than I had anticipated, but this was due to the success of the program and associated work. This was manifested in several ways: for example, the interview with the policeman, scheduled for one hour, lasted all afternoon, and it took a long time to read and sort through the many newspaper cuttings about thefts which the pupils brought in. The little plays they acted out also took some time: one group of girls, who wouldn't normally say boo to a goose, acted out a very comical play indeed and brought the house down. Another slight delay was caused when I had to order a project collection from the School Library Service on robbers and pirates, because there was such a rush on our school library books.

There is little doubt in my mind that the computer contributed a great deal towards the success of this series of lessons – indeed, the scheme was based entirely around the computer program MALLORY. Apart from the written work they produced, the opportunities it provided for problem-solving talk and individual and group research were invaluable. I had used virtually all of these types of activity before in other contexts, but rarely have they worked as well.

CONCLUSIONS

It is apparent from these two brief case studies that using the computer as part of a scheme of work, whether it forms the basis of the work or merely one part, can bring benefits for the teacher. It can be seen that both relate to otherwise 'traditional' work, but that the pupils in both cases appeared to be far more enthusiastic when the computer was used. This could be interpreted as sheer novelty value, which will disappear when the computer becomes as ordinary in a Language Arts classroom as a book, and it is possible to foresee a situation when pupils begin to say, 'Oh no! Not the computer again!' However, this is some time away and will depend, to a great extent, upon how the computer is used and what software is employed in the meantime. Hopefully, before our pupils have a chance to find the computer 'ordinary', software will have been developed which will replace any novelty value with an imaginative stimulation of genuine interest. Some programs of that nature have been mentioned elsewhere in this book and more is in development.

However, it is worth mentioning at this point that I used MALLORY with a group of first years as an end-of-term relaxation. I had 'customized' it and used members of staff at the school as suspects. It was a complete failure. It failed to engage the pupils on any level, apart from an initial, brief interest. The group with which I used it had not been over-exposed to the computer and showed a great deal of interest when they entered the room and saw the computer set up for them to use. The explanation for their lack of interest in the work can therefore only be that either the program was bad or that the context of its use was wrong. We have seen in the second case study that the program was received very well by that class, so that leaves only the context of its use – a 'one-off' lesson. I have had quite a few 'failures' with the computer and, looking back, most have been failures because of the *context* in which the computer has been used. It is my contention, therefore, that computer programs, if they are to be employed successfully, demand to be integrated into a scheme of work and that one measure of a program's worth is whether it lends itself to being so or not.

It is this idea of context which ensures that the teacher as an essential element in education is not threatened by the new technology, because it is only the teacher's skill which can provide a suitable context for its use. It is a two-edged sword, however, for the teaching profession could cause the demise of the computer as a liberating force in education by using it indiscriminately.

8

FUTURE PERFECT?

The only way to predict the future is to
have power to shape the future.
(Eric Hoffer, *The Passionate
State of Mind*)

As with many machines and inventions throughout history, the computer is a machine which will have an impact that can only be truly assessed with the advantage of hindsight: any predictions or crystal-ball-gazing can be nothing more than pure speculation. Nevertheless, I would like to conclude with a few observations on the future of computers both in the Language Arts and in education generally. However, it may be apposite first to widen the scope of the previous chapters and consider how the computer can be integrated into the school, both at departmental level and in terms of the whole school.

First steps – towards a departmental policy

I have stressed elsewhere that the purchase and use of a computer in the teaching of the Language Arts should be a departmental decision and that much of the work which needs to be done to integrate the computer into the syllabus should be formed into departmental policy. The reasons for these assertions are twofold: to ensure a consistent approach over the department and so that teaching strategies may be developed from a coherent statement of policy. The benefits of arriving at an agreed policy are not only in achieving one, however: the discussion necessary to do so can often be stimulating and rewarding in its own right and will, as we have seen during this book, get right to the heart of what we call 'English'. It is not my purpose to propose a particular policy, for that will depend upon the context of the school and the wishes of the department. I would, however, like to suggest, albeit very briefly, ways in which this policy can be arrived at, noting on the way that the English Department in any school has an important part to play in the development of a whole-school computer policy.

It may well be that each department has an agreed syllabus which will, in the secondary school, reflect an emphasis on examination preparation in the last two years of compulsory education and a more general approach for younger pupils. That syllabus will, no doubt, mention specific areas of the Language Arts, various courses or books which will be used and, perhaps, particular approaches which will be utilized in achieving the aims of the syllabus. However, I wonder how often teachers within the department actually look at the syllabus when planning sequences of lessons, and how often the syllabus is revised? With the advent of a computer, a whole new area of teaching strategies is opened up as well as new skills for the teacher and the pupil to learn: it is then vital for the departmental syllabus to be revised to reflect the changes if the syllabus is to mean anything at all.

There are two ways in which this could be achieved: by 'tinkering' with the old syllabus and inserting paragraphs here and there, or by starting from scratch and reformulating the department's aims, objectives and methodology. I am sure my tone has indicated that I favour the latter approach which, although causing a great deal more work, will be a far more meaningful statement of the direction a department is taking. The former approach would, no doubt, be effected by the Head of Department with or without the assistance of others and would result, I believe, in the syllabus becoming something filed away and rarely looked at. This would occur because few teachers in the department would have any stake in it, they would not be involved in determining its content nor any philosophical views implicit in such a document. Unfortunately, I fear that this happens in far too many schools.

If it is decided to start from scratch again, there are strategies which will help to make the process less time-consuming. One good source of ideas for such strategies is 'The English Department Book' by the ILEA English Centre (1982), which also contains suggestions as to how to focus discussion on important areas. The model suggested involves 'seeing the syllabus as a developing, re-negotiable manual-and-manifesto, rather than a once-and-for-all wad' which is arrived at by:

> a series of excursions, led by different people in the department, starting from and coming back to problems which the department identifies. . . . Assumptions which emerge in the course of excursions need to become explicit views: the framework of attitudes and principles which make bits of practice coherent.
>
> (Marigold and Simons, 1982, 75)

Five levels of questioning are suggested:

Level One: What kind of child would we ideally like to see emerge from five years of English teaching?

Level Two: What role does English play in the development of children's use of language?

Level Three: What is the proper stuff of English?

Level Four: How is one year's work in English different from the next?

Level Five: What happens in practice?

These seem to me to be excellent starting points, and, of course, there is no reason, when seen in this light, for the production of a syllabus to be a one-man show – it becomes a joint responsibility and thus the property of the whole department. Considered in this way, the new demands made by computers and how the latter can aid the teacher will not be separated from the wider aims of what the department as a whole is trying to deal with but will become an organic part of it.

This is, of course, not something which can be done quickly and it will need revision in the light of experience. The lesson assessments I mentioned in Chapter 6 would be a key part of the formulation of the new syllabus – especially if, as will be likely, the computer is used in the department's teaching before the new syllabus is in any sort of shape. Whilst this will be a reasonably long-term aim, perhaps a year, perhaps more, every opportunity should be taken to ensure that at least one member of the department is released to attend in-service training with computers whenever such courses are being run and it need not be the same person every time: indeed, for only one person to attend all the courses would be limiting the department's response to computers. It is sometimes difficult to arrange to release teachers to attend in-service training, particularly when most local authorities are very reluctant to provide supply teachers to cover such absences, but it is difficult to know how else a department is supposed to progress.

There are other ways, however, of keeping abreast of developments. There are a number of journals which can supply useful information (see Reference Section II), subscriptions to which will not stretch the department's finances too much. There are also interest groups on a local and national level (see Reference Section IV), which can provide interchanges of ideas and information. If there are no local groups in existence, then there is no reason why such groups should not be formed. In fact, there are such forums in existence in every part of the country for secondary schools in the shape of CSE Consortia – perhaps a discussion about computers at one of the regular meetings could be the starting point for a working party in that field for the local area.

Links with feeder schools are also important in the forma-
tion of policy. There should be a degree of co-ordination in the
approach to computers and how they are used (if they *are*
used), as well as, possibly, knowledge about which programs
are being used: it is perhaps confusing for pupils who come
from junior or middle schools where the computer is used
frequently for a large variety of purposes to be placed in
secondary schools where they do not see any computers at all.
A policy for the secondary school which pays no attention to
feeder schools can only be regarded as lacking in an important
element. Similarly, the parents must be considered, too.
Teachers are having to learn the new skills associated with
computers because their concern is with education, but
parents' experience of computers will be only in relation to
other aspects of their use, such as in the parents' jobs or as a
games machine at home. Some may be suspicious of computers
being used in the teaching of the Language Arts, perhaps
believing that their own experience is all that there is to
computers. They will need to be informed about how computers are being used and why, and it is important, obviously, for
the department to realize that fully before they can inform the
parents.

THE SCHOOL CONTEXT

As early as 1921, it was acknowledged that the subject
'English' had a central role in schools generally, and both the
Newbolt Report and George Sampson, one of the members of
the Committee, stated that year that every teacher is a teacher
of English, a point taken up again more recently in a blaze of
publicity in the Bullock Report, giving rise to the more precise
concept of 'Language Across the Curriculum', although its
meaning in practice differs from school to school. The dangers
inherent in this concept are expressed well by Allen:

> The subject English has extended its boundaries into
> language, so that many English teachers see no need to

distinguish between the kind of work that is done in English lessons and the language element in all learning. Indeed, I have heard English teachers express a loss of interest in English as a subject and a preference to involve themselves with wider curricular matters – language across the curriculum or language in learning.

(Allen, 1980, 97)

He argues that, while the diverse elements English has taken on board have produced a wealth of ideas, there is a danger that we might lose sight of those essential elements of the subject: not just literature and not just language, but a balance between them. This is a point well worth bearing in mind when considering the role of the Language Arts in the development of a whole-school policy for computers because we can offer more to other departments than just a consideration of the place of language in learning.

Most of the programs I have mentioned in this book do not relate just to the subject English, but draw on other disciplines in their content or can be used in other subjects. Examples of this are QUEST, the information retrieval package which can be used in the sciences or the humanities, MARY ROSE, which draws upon maths, geography and history as well as on the Language Arts, and TRAY, which could contain texts in any language. It is therefore obvious that, when using computers, there is common ground between the subjects on the timetable, but that this common ground is far more than just linguistic. It is purely the linguistic element, I would argue, that has formed the *raison d'être* of some of the integration of subjects, especially in the lower part of secondary schools. In connection with this, Allen makes what I feel is a very valuable observation:

It is for what it can *contribute* to other areas that English might join together in integrated work, as well as what we might gain; we contribute nothing if we are not clear what we are doing. We can make connections with art, music, humanities, biology, and we can support the concern with language in schools. This must be done, however, from a clear grasp of the priorities in English.

(Allen, 1980, 134)

It is clear, then, that we must not make the mistake of allowing ourselves to believe that the common ground between subjects is the totality of the Language Arts – it is only one area of our concern.

The unique contribution that computers can make to the integration of subjects, and, indeed, to the subjects themselves, is in providing a focus which has more to do with process than content, more to do with learning strategies than with language. Using computers as the linking factor between subjects therefore takes away the purely language-oriented contribution which subject English has provided in the past. It opens the way for teachers of the Language Arts to examine the nature of the conceptual contributions they can make, involving, perhaps, considerations of aesthetics, values and morals – concepts which may have been given less prominence than language by teachers of English in integrated studies. It would, perhaps, be claiming rather too much to say that no other subject shares an interest in these concepts, yet it is possible to say that the Language Arts approaches them in a manner uniquely its own, and this is why the Language Arts teacher has an important role in the development of a policy for computers across the school.

Towards a school policy for computers

While I would advocate the overhauling of a subject syllabus in order to take account of the potential of the computer in that subject area, I would not necessarily advocate similar measures for the school curriculum, although it does seem to me to be an excellent opportunity to do just that. Instead, I think that it should be possible to develop an overall school policy that regards computers as a natural extension of the departmental syllabus review outlined above. That there is a need for such a policy is, I believe, without question; otherwise, for example, a pupil could be faced with several types of computer around the school for no apparent rhyme or reason, or using exactly the same program in different manners but in an uncoordinated way. The school in which I teach has only a few computers, but it is generally realized that before we buy any more we ought to develop some sort of policy so that we are all 'pulling in the same direction'.

There must be many ways in which to approach the formulation of a whole-school policy, but I do feel that there are certain constants. In any school, but more especially in large schools, there is a need to appoint someone who will have an overview of developments within the school and who will be assigned to monitor and co-ordinate the computer policy. This is necessary because the field of computers in education is growing quickly and, aside from keeping their 'finger on the pulse' of such new developments and disseminating information about them to the appropriate staff, it is important that someone has a complete view of computer use within the school rather than a fragmented, department-based one. This person would also be responsible for maintaining another constant – the school software library. This, as I envisage it, would be a central store of all the programs used within the school (most software allows a 'back-up' copy to be taken for use within the establishment which purchased it), so that stock is not duplicated, and staff have easy access to computer programs used elsewhere in the school.

The third constant must be consultation on the widest possible basis, in order to take into account the many, no doubt differing, interests of the various departments. Perhaps one of the best ways to achieve this consultation would be to form a working party made up of one teacher from each department, or group of departments, who have previously had discussions within their departments, preferably arising out of a syllabus review. Of course, it would be best if all members of the working party had experience of using the computer in the teaching of their subject, but, in any case, each member of the working party should be delegated to investigate the available software in their subject.

Once formed, the working party could examine areas of common interest and need and could work towards a cohesive policy statement. On the way, they could consider such questions as:

i) Why do we wish to use computers and how can the curriculum reflect this?

ii) What can the school/the pupils/the staff gain from using computers?

iii) How will they be used?

iv) Should we invest in only one make of computer?

v) Do we create a computer room?

vi) Where will they be kept? Will they be safe?

vii) Can we anticipate future needs and work towards them?

viii) Should we teach programming?

ix) What provisions can be made for in-service training?

x) How do other schools in the locality use computers? Can we learn from them?

This is not, nor is it intended to be, a complete or prescriptive list – merely some starting points for discussion.

Towards the future

Throughout this book, I have been at pains to point out the dangers of 'going overboard' with the computer and that it should be regarded as a tool, albeit a very powerful and flexible one. I have come to characterize this danger as 'The Black-Headed Gull Syndrome': one or two of my colleagues (who know about these things) assure me that the black-headed gull exhibits a very strange behaviour when presented with a square, man-made egg beside its own in its nest. Rather than sit on its own eggs, the gull will attempt to hatch the square egg to the extent of allowing its own eggs to remain unhatched. It seems to me that educational computing has, for some people, been a similar exercise – suddenly 'converted' to computers, they develop tunnel vision and all of their normally balanced views of their educational aims, objectives and methodology become subsumed into an overwhelming desire to show pupils, friends and colleagues that the computer is the deity of the 1980s. They are aided in this by the aggressive advertising of the computer and software manufacturers who take every opportunity to turn everyone's (and especially children's) natural awe into something akin to reverence.

In a sense, however, they are doing the cause of educational computing an important service, because a slight cynicism about innovation is a useful tool in a teacher's armoury. Teachers are now justifiably asking exactly how the computer can be integrated into their subject in a way which will bring most benefit to their pupils: as one of my colleagues once put it – 'As a Head of Department, if you ask me to spend £800 on a computer, I will refuse: I'd rather spend it on a new set of textbooks.' While those who believe that computers should be a vital part of the educative process may find this akin to heresy, it is an entirely understandable attitude from someone who has been teaching for a number of years and has established a methodology and rationale of teaching which has proved effective. This is, without doubt, causing those who are con- vinced of the computer's value to examine carefully the role of computers in education generally, and in subject areas specifically: this book can be seen as part of this process in action.

Strangely enough, it is because of this that I see the future of computing in the Language Arts optimistically. Teachers in this area have been traditionally involved in humanistic and aesthetic areas of development and much of the prescriptive writing in 'English' over the past 100 years or so has been concerned with protecting and enriching 'culture' through the teaching of the subject, releasing children's creative abilities and helping them to learn to communicate effectively in all modes of language. As Mathieson puts it:

> The content and tone of discussion about the aims of English teaching during the past 150 years testify to its supporters' view that the subject is of special importance in pupils' lives. Prescriptive writing insists upon the need for exceptionally gifted people to take on this responsibility, and, on occasions, it goes as far as to claim that neglect of drama, or creativity, or literature, will stultify pupils' personal development or precipitate cultural catastrophe.
>
> (Mathieson, 1975, 193)

It could be argued that 'English' has been child-centred from the start, whereas other subjects have come late to it, or have never arrived at all. In this sense, therefore, teachers of the Language Arts will be more likely to approach the computer from what I believe to be the only defensible standpoint – how will *the children* benefit from using the computer in their learning? Given the picture of the teaching of 'English' painted by Mathieson, this will come more easily to teachers of the Language Arts than perhaps any other body of teachers – although I anticipate screams of anguish from some quarters about that statement! However, if teachers of the Language Arts become actively involved in the use of computers in education, I feel that our pupils can only benefit.

How, then, will this happen? Many practising teachers are already starting to use the computer in their teaching, but have the difficulty of coming to terms with an unfamiliar technology before they can see the potential of the computer as a learning tool. However, we are starting to see student teachers going through college and university who are already familiar with the technology, and some who already take it for granted. For them, the computer will be just as natural an aid to teaching as the tape recorder, or OHP, or video has been for previous generations. Upon taking up appointments, their effect on schools will be gradual but inevitable as their older colleagues begin to see for themselves how computers can be used to enhance learning. This assumes, of course, that teacher-training establishments do actually make some provision for a consideration of how computers can be used – and they are making such provisions, gradually: one university has recently announced that it intends to issue every student with a personal microcomputer (a Sinclair QL) and many other further-education establishments will, no doubt, be watching to see the results of this experiment.

Most local authorities now have advisers appointed to over-see the development of computer use in schools – Staffordshire has no less than sixteen advisory teachers for this purpose. This is coupled with the in-service training which is being provided by most education authorities now for serving teachers. The original Department of Industry scheme for the purchase of computers included the stipulation that each school purchas-ing a computer under the scheme should send two teachers on a training course to learn how to use it. In some parts of the country, this stipulation has already been met, in others it is in the process of being met – and there is now a large number of teachers who have at least some familiarity with the computer. How many of these are teachers of the Language Arts is not known, but I would suspect that the number is very small. It is vital, therefore, that the professional organizations concerned – principally, in this case, the National Association for the Teaching of English (NATE) – play an increasingly important part in disseminating information and providing support for the classroom teacher, especially as the Microelectronics Education Programme (charged with those duties, among others) reaches 'the end of the road' in March 1986. Again, this is being done with the creation of a NATE Working Party on Computers which arose directly out of the proceedings of their National Conferences in Guildford in 1983 and in Durham in 1984. We are, therefore, seeing all of the relevant bodies – universities, teacher-training establishments, professional organizations and local education authorities – becoming involved in the process of 'consciousness-raising' and training, both generally, in the wider field of education, and specifically, in the Language Arts.

We are still dependent, though, upon the production of good quality software, for without it the computer is just a useless pile of junk. Many large publishers are gradually withdrawing from developing programs for education because of the small returns available. Some are turning to programs which will sell in the home market as well as in schools; others are 'consolidating' their lists and will end up with a greatly reduced number of programs for sale. If we were to rely purely upon these larger publishers, we would find ourselves in the situation in which American teachers find themselves: in the USA the only ideas developed into programs by publishers tend to be those which can be proved to have the potential for high-volume sales. It must be hoped, therefore, that other sources can be found, which do not necessarily put such a high premium on profit. A possible avenue to explore here is the contribution that certain local authorities are making to the development of good software: Oxfordshire and Suffolk are two good examples. In addition, smaller companies such as CLASS and Netherhall Software are beginning to produce programs for education which have a great deal to offer. I have heard criticisms of this 'cottage-industry' situation, but I consider that, at this time, this is the only way in which teachers can guarantee some control over what is being produced and ensure that good ideas are turned into software. Clearly, the DES shares this view, for it has been announced that, following the end of the Microelectronics Education Programme in 1986, money will be available for software development until 1989 – one only hopes that it will be the 'cottage industry' which is funded and that the funding will be sufficient. Even if my hopes in this direction are not totally fulfilled, however, the programs I have mentioned in this book – and others yet to be released – still provide a valuable resource for the teaching of the Language Arts and, I have no doubt, will retain their value for some time to come.

The computers themselves are, of course, developing all the time and four years from the release of the most widely used computers in schools today, we are being told that they are obsolete and that it is the new sixteen-bit computer (such as the RML Nimbus) in which we should be investing our money. In four years' time, who is to say that sixteen-bit technology will not be obsolete? Some would say that this does present a real problem for teachers, but I would say that the problem is greatly overstated. Schools which have RML 480Zs or BBC B computers will not suddenly lose all their software overnight, nor will that software suddenly lose all its educational value, nor will the computers themselves suddenly be consigned to the stock cupboard for ever. No, these computers will still have a part to play in five, even ten, years' time even if their role is restricted in the light of later acquisitions and developments. True, the newer computers may be able to carry out their functions more efficiently and, perhaps, impressively, but what is far more important is whether we are using the computers we actually have in education in the most effective manner: our attention should be on the child, not the computer.

One major obstacle to the full integration of the computer into the Language Arts, and education in general, must be the domination of the secondary-school curriculum (and, by extension, primary-school curricula) by examinations. It would be, I suppose, rather naïve and idealistic to hope that the spectre of exams will cease to loom large in the minds of teachers, pupils and parents, but I do not believe that it is too much to hope that examination boards will, in time, change to welcome the new technology. I feel that the government and examination boards have wasted a great opportunity to revitalize education in their supposedly new proposals for the GCSE, which are, in practice, simply a reworking of the old dual system and, as far as the Language Arts are concerned, a rehashing of the same old examination elements of essay-writing, comprehension tests [*sic*] and letter/report writing with the added bonus of a compulsory oral element which some schools are already trying to make optional. I am informed that work which has been word-processed will not be acceptable (even in coursework), nor will the production of a database from a set text be allowed, despite the fact that this calls for as much understanding of the text, if not more, than the standard essay: in fact, nowhere do the proposals encourage teachers to adopt new methods or approaches to the Language Arts. Despite that, I gain the impression from talking to other teachers that innovation is taking place and that examination boards are being frustrated in their insistence on methods of assessment which reward the Gradgrind approach to education, and this fuels my optimism for the future. What must happen, of course, is that teachers must lobby the examination boards at every opportunity – even those who do not use the computer in their teaching, or who are not yet convinced of its worth, must give those who are using the computer (and their pupils) a 'fair crack of the whip'.

I have also heard it said that the parlous state of funding of education will frustrate the introduction of computers into schools in any great number. Whilst it is true to say that education is being squeezed so much that even the HMIs have started to complain, it is also true to say that almost every school in Britain has at least one computer and that prices of computers are falling, especially those which have been superseded, such as the BBC B, the price of which is now rapidly dropping to the cost of a set of textbooks. I hope that in this book I have shown how one computer can be utilized effectively in a classroom, and I have little hesitation in saying that future funding need not prevent computers from being used in the Language Arts: we may have to fight a little harder for access to the machine, but teachers of the Language Arts have a much better claim than many to its use. Of course, I am not saying that we do not need more investment in new technology in our schools. I am saying that we already have enough with which to start to create a solid foundation of theory and practice from which we can build when we have the resources to expand computer provision in schools generally.

I see the future, therefore, as evolution rather than revolution, and am far happier to see it that way around: revolutions have a nasty habit of going sour. One of the strengths of the developing use of computers in the Language Arts is that the impetus is coming from classroom teachers and is not being imposed on them, something which is, perhaps, rare in the field of educational innovation. The fact that the new technology is being implemented only gradually in the Language Arts, and that the demand for it is coming from the 'chalk face', gives good reason to believe that the computer is here to stay: as I see it, that is beyond doubt already. However, in order to ensure that the computer becomes a *positive* force, rather than merely another hurdle between our pupils and a liberating education, we need to be very clear in our own minds exactly why we are using it *before* we use it. The computer thus presents teachers with a clear challenge and a unique opportunity for change: with the exercise of careful planning, considered methodologies and, above all, imagination, the future may not be perfect, but it will certainly be better for our pupils.

PART THREE:
REFERENCE SECTION

I

BOOKS AND ARTICLES REFERRED
TO IN THE TEXT

Adams, A. and Jones, E. (1983) *Teaching Humanities in the Microelectronic Age*, Milton Keynes, Open University Press

Allen, D. (1980) *English Teaching Since 1965*, London, Heinemann

Chandler, D. (1982) *Micro Primer: Study Text*, Loughborough, Tecmedia

Chandler, D. (1984) *Young Learners and the Microcomputer*, Milton Keynes, Open University Press

Chandler, D. (ed.) (1983) *Exploring English with Microcomputers*, London, Council for Educational Technology

Hammond, R. (1984) *Computers and Your Child,* London, Century

Horner, S. (ed.) (1983) *Best Laid Plans: English Teachers at Work*, Harlow, Longman for Schools Council

Lunzer, E. and Gardner, K. (1979) *The Effective Use of Reading*, London, Heinemann

Marcus, S. (1983) 'Real-Time Gadgets with Feedback' in *The Writing Instructor*, Summer 1983, 2 (4)

Marigold, R. and Simons, M. (1982) *The English Department Handbook*, London, ILEA English Centre

Mathieson, M. (1975) *The Preachers of Culture*, London, George Allen & Unwin

Papert, S. (1980) *Mindstorms*, Brighton, Harvester Press

Royce, R. (1984) 'Educational Software Publishing', in *Computers in the Teaching of English*, 1 (2)

Scottish Examinations Board (1984) *Standard Grade Arrangements in English*, Edinburgh, Scottish Examinations Board

Stewart-Dore, J. (1983) *ERICA* in *English in Australia*, March 1983 (63)

Walsh, W. (1959) *The Use of Imagination*, Harmondsworth, Penguin

Wilkinson, A. (1965) *Spoken English*, Birmingham, Birmingham University Press

II
SUGGESTIONS FOR FURTHER READING

Books

Chandler, D. and Marcus, S. (ed.) (1985) *Computers and Literacy*, Milton Keynes, Open University Press

Daines, D. (1984) *Databases in the Classroom*, Tunbridge Wells, Castle House

Higgins, J. and Johns, T. (1984) *Computers in Language Learning*, London, Collins ELT

Robinson, B. (1985) *Microcomputers and the Language Arts*, Milton Keynes, Open University Press

Terry, C. (ed.) (1984) *Using Microcomputers in Schools*, Beckenham, Croom Helm

Periodicals

Educational Computing (monthly) Priory Court, 30–32 Farringdon Lane, London EC1R 3AU

Computers In Schools (four issues per year) MUSE, PO Box 43, Hull HU1 2HD

Computers In the Teaching of English (four issues per year)

71 Germander Place, Conniburrow, Milton Keynes MK14 7DW

Journal of Computer Assisted Learning (three issues per year) Blackwell Scientific Publications Ltd, PO Box 88, Oxford

Primary Teaching and Micros, Scholastic Publications Ltd, Leamington Spa, Warwickshire CV32 4DG

III
COMPUTER SOFTWARE AND HARDWARE

Programs referred to in the text

For addresses of sources, see IV

Name	Source	Computer	Comments
ADDVERSE	CLASS	BBC	An excellent word animator.
CLASS READERS	CLASS	BBC	A variety of programs, including a version of TRAY, with a range of purposes.
CLASS WRITER	CLASS	BBC	A utility program for storing text.
DATAVIEW	Suffolk LEA	RML	A teletext simulator, ideal as an introduction to this type of database.

Name	Source	Computer	Comments
EDWORD	Clwyd Technics Ltd	BBC	One of the most widely used word processors for the BBC.
EDFAX	Tecmedia	BBC	A local viewdata system.
FACTFILE	Cambridge Micro Software	RML/BBC	A simple database program.
MALLORY	MEP	RML/BBC	A simulation of a theft, which can be 'customized' to a certain extent.
MARY ROSE	Ginn & Co.	RML/BBC	A simulation of the raising of the flagship *Mary Rose*.
NEWSDESK	SMDP	BBC	In development.
QUEST	AUCBE	RML/BBC	A very powerful database program.
SAQQARA	Ginn & Co.	BBC/RML	A superb simulation of an archaeological dig in Egypt.
SPACEX	4mat Educational Software	BBC/RML	A space-adventure game.
STORYMAKER	Chelsea College	BBC	Undergoing field trials.
TELETEXT	RML	RML	A viewdata simulator, as yet only available in black and white.
THE HOBBIT	Melbourne House	BBC	An adventure game based on the Tolkien book.
TRAY	ILECC/CLASS MEP	BBC/RML	The MEP version is free to all who attend the courses which use the MEP Primary Language Pack.
WORDPLAY	MEP	BBC/RML	A program, included in the Primary Language Pack, which patterns

Name	Source	Computer	Comments
			words provided by the user.
WORDWISE	Computer Concepts	BBC	One of the more popular word processors for the BBC: available as a ROM-pack.
WRITE	Oxfordshire LEA	RML	An excellent word processor designed for school use.

Hardware

Name	Source	Computer	Comments
BBC B+ Computer	Acorn/ Vector Marketing	BBC B	One of the more popular computers with a wide range of software available; however the BBC B is no longer available.
Concept Keyboard	Star Microterminals Ltd	BBC/RML	A large board with touch-sensitive areas and overlays, which enables the computer to be used without having necessarily to use the keyboard.
Disc drives	Various	BBC	An ever-growing number of suppliers for these. The most popular appear to be 'Cumana' drives, but check with local advisers.
Disc drives	Research Machines Ltd	RML	RML produce their own drives and it is probably best to use theirs if using an RML computer.

Name	Source	Computer	Comments
Microwriter and Quinkey	Microwriter Ltd	BBC/RML	Hand-held text compiler which in the case of the Quinkey is attached to the computer by cable. A useful alternative to the ordinary keyboard.
Printers	Various	BBC/RML	A large number of suppliers and not all printers will suit all types of computer or be suitable for all purposes. Check with the local adviser.
VDU/ Monitors	Various	BBC/RML	Many suppliers: check with your local adviser.
380Z, 480Z and Nimbus	Research Machines Ltd	380Z, 480Z and Nimbus	Bigger memory than the BBC but more expensive. The Nimbus is new and untried as yet. Good 'upgrade path'.

IV

USEFUL ADDRESSES

Suppliers of Software and Hardware

4Mat Educational Software, Linden Lea, Rock Park, Barnstaple, Devon EX32 9AQ

Acornsoft, 4a Market Hill, Cambridge CB2 3NJ

AUCBE (Advisory Unit for Computer-Based Education), Endymion Road, Hatfield, Herts AL10 8AU

Cambridge Micro Software, Cambridge University Press, Shaftesbury Road, Cambridge CB2 2RU

CLASS (Cambridge Language Arts Software Services), 197 Henley Road, Caversham, Reading RG4 0LJ

Clwyd Technics Ltd, Antelope Industrial Estate, Rhydymwyn, Mold, Clwyd

Computer Concepts, 16 Wayside, Chipperfield, Herts

Computers in the Curriculum Project, Chelsea College, University of London, Hudson Building, 552 Kings Road, London SW10 0UA

Ginn & Co. Ltd, Prebendal House, Parsons Fee, Aylesbury, Bucks HP20 2QZ

ILECC (Inner London Educational Computing Centre), Centre for Learning Resources, 275 Kennington Lane, London SE11 5QZ

Longman Micro Software, Longman Group Resources Unit, 33–35 Tanner Row, York YO1 1JP

Melbourne House, Church Yard, Tring, Herts HP25 5LU

Microwriter Ltd, 31 Southampton Row, London WC1

MUSE, PO Box 43, Hull HU1 2HD

Oxfordshire LEA, Microtechnology Advisory Group, Macclesfield House, New Road, Oxford OX1 1NA

Research Machines Ltd, Mill Street, Oxford OX2 0BW

SMDP (Scottish Microelectronics Development Programme), 74 Victoria Crescent Road, Glasgow G12 9JN

Star Microterminals, 22 Hyde Street, Winchester, Hants SO23 7DR

Suffolk LEA, Mike Treadaway, Advisory Teacher, Area Education Office, Suffolk House, London Road North, Lowestoft NR32 1BH

Tecmedia Ltd, 5 Granby Street, Loughborough LE11 3DU

Vector Marketing, Dennington Estate, Wellingborough, Northants NN8 2RL

INTEREST GROUPS IN THE AREA OF
THE LANGUAGE ARTS

All names and addresses are current as of December 1985. Those organizations marked with an asterisk are exclusively concerned with the Language Arts.

Birmingham Educational Computing Centre, The Bordesley Centre, Camp Hill, Stratford Road, Birmingham B11 1AR

*CAL in English Working Party, c/o Karen Rigby, Highfields School, Boundary Way, Penn, Wolverhampton, Staffs

Cleveland Educational Computing Centre, Prissick Base, Marton Road, Middlesborough TS4 3RZ

Havant Schools Microelectronic Programme, Software Refer-

ence Library, Wakeford School, Wakefords Way, Havant
PO9 5JL

*MATE (Micro Applications in the Teaching of English), c/o
Joan Ashton, Edgbarrow School, Crowthorne, Berks.

MEDU (Microelectronics Education Development Unit),
Bishop Grosseteste College, Newport, Lincoln LN1 3DY

*MICE (Microcomputers in the Curriculum for English), 71
Germander Place, Conniburrow, Milton Keynes MK14
7DW

*Micros in English Working Party, c/o Richard Pugh,
Mainholm Academy, Mainholm Road, Ayr, Ayrshire

*MIDGET (Microcomputer Development by Glasgow English
Teachers), c/o Andy Heron, Possilpark Secondary School,
32 Carbeth Street, Glasgow, Lanarks

*NATE Computer Working Party, 49 Broomgrove Road,
Sheffield S10 2NA

*Sunderland English and Microcomputer Group, c/o Jerry
Fitzgibbon, Monkwearmouth School, Torver Crescent,
Seaburndene, Sunderland

GENERAL INDEX

References in bold-face type indicate a definition or explanation of the term.

ACORNSOFT 10, 166
adventure games **44**, 48, 50, 51, 56, 69, 71, 72, 124, 128, 144
advisory staff, role of 123, 133, 165, 166
arcade games xii, 4, 5, 6, 12, 14
'authoring systems' 14, **15**

Bullock Report 129, 158

CEEFAX 76–8, 80
CLASS 9, 11, 166
classroom layout 112–14, 131, 143
computers
  and control 11, 14, 15, 31, 65, 111, 112, 114, 122, 128, 129
  and traditional skills xii, 16, 17, 38, 46, 67, 115, 130
  attitudes to xii, 3, 4, 9, 106, 107, 126, 158, 162, 163
  choice of 96–9, 167
  departmental policy on 96, 108, 123, 154–8
  modes of use 27, 122, 128–30
  ownership of, 4, 5, 9, 38, 97, 114
  school policy on 18, 96, 105, 116, 155, 159–62
  security 103, 104
  threat of xii, 15, 114, 129, 153
'computer literacy' 17, 18, 96, 111, 115, 116
computer room 35, 104, 105, 162
cross-curricular links 10, 85, 86, 92, 126, 158–61

databases **7**, 42, 43, 78–82, 84, 85, 89, 168
  construction of 49, 81, 82, 84–8, 90
decision-making 7, 48, 51, 68, 69, 70
disc 25, 99, **100**, 101, 121

discussion 48, 49, 54, 64, 65, 69, 71, 86, 128, 136, 138, 139, 142, 155
'download' **81**

evaluation
  of lessons 124, 130, 131, 157
  of reading 40, 41
  of software 10, 108–10, 116, 120, 131
  of talk 59–63, 73, 132
  of writing 21, 22, 29, 131, 132
examinations xiii, 18, 24, 38, 40, 41, 59–63, 73, 155, 167, 168

grammar 37, 143
groupings of pupils 64, 65, 86, 89, 112, 122, 127–31

hard copy **7**, 103

imagination xiv, 19, 69, 123, 169
information (*see also* databases)
  growth of 75, 76
  importance of 12, 75, 76
  systems: CEEFAX/ORACLE 76–8, 80; PRESTEL 76–81, 88–90
in-service training 106, 107, 120, 133, 157, 161, 165, 166
'interactive' 50, **51**, 52, 56, 80
ITMA 73

keyboard
  alternatives: Concept 103, **118**; Mouse 103, **118**; Quinkey 36, 97, **117**, 118, 119; QWERTY 23, 36, 117
  skills 87, 110, 114–16, 140

language development 8, 36, 37, 42, 52

learning strategies 12, 14, 42, 47, 52, 92, 120, 160
lesson
  evaluation 124, 130–2, 157
  preparation 119, 120, 122, 123, 126, 131, 135, 144
literacy, changing definition of 17, 18, 38, 55–8, 67
literature xiii, 42, 49, 90, 91

modem **79**
monitor (*see also* VDU) 23, 25, 26, 28, 36, 45, 102, 113

NATE 165
Netherhall Software 166
networks 27, **35**, 70, 98, 99, 104, 105
Newbolt Report 158

ORACLE 76–8, 80
oracy 59–63, 73, 74

peripherals **102**, 103
play 5, 72, 107, 121
poetry, 32–4
PRESTEL 76–81, 88–90
printer 24, 25, 35, 46, 72, 89, 103
problem solving 7, 48, 52, 84
programming 6, 9, 14, 15, 33, 121
prose 27–32

RAM **100**
reading
  and motivation 44, 45, 52, 56
  comprehension 40, 41, 48, 51, 52, 57, 61, 168
  'ERICA' 46–9
  evaluation of 40, 41
  links with writing 34, 49–50
  nature of 44, 45, 55–8
  styles of 41, 46
role play 51, 68, 70

ROM **100**, 101

simulations **7**, 68–70, 71
software
    development 9, 11, 15, 43, 66, 67,
        132, 166
    evaluation 10, 108–10, 116, 120,
        131
    interactive 50, **51**, 52, 80
    support material 110, 122, 129,
        131
speech
    recognition **66**, 67, 117
    synthesis 38, 55, **66**, 67
stories, multiple plot 17, 29–31, 50,
    52

talk
    assessment of, 59–63, 73
    discussion 48, 49, 54, 64, 65, 69,
        71, 86, 128, 136, 138, 139,
        142, 155

exploratory nature 63, 69
    management of 60, 64, 65, 72
    promotion of 59, 70–4, 84
technophobia **106**, 107, 132
Telesoftware **80**

VDU (*see also* monitor) **102**
videotext **21**, 57

word processing **6**, 16, 25, 26, 27,
        35, 38, 45, 46, 50, 117, 129,
        168
writing
    aids 7, 17, 25, 26, 36, 37, 57
    collaborative 17, 34–6, 70
    evaluation of 21, 22, 29, 131, 132
    'invisible' **28**
    links with reading 34, 49–50
    presentation of 22, 23, 24, 26
    process 22, 24, 28, 29, 50
    traditional skills of 7, 16, 20, 21,
        22, 24, 38, 39, 67, 114–16

NAME INDEX

Adams, A. 38, 67, 76
Allen, D. 59, 60, 61, 62, 73, 158, 159

Chandler, D. xv, 5, 12, 15, 24, 43, 69, 75, 77, 81, 84, 92, 109

Gardner, K. 41, 44, 50, 55, 56, 57, 58

Hammond, R. 5
Horner, S. 119
Hunter-Watts, P. xv

Kay, A. 16

Lunzer, E. 41, 44, 50, 55, 56, 57, 58

Marcus, S. 20, 28
Mason, S. xv
Mathieson, M. 164
McGough, R. 33
McLuhan, M. 55
Melton, J. 123

Moy, B. 52

Papert, S. 8, 23
Philips, R. 45
Pugh, R. 71

Robinson, B. 32
Royce, R. 9

Sampson, G. 158
Sawford, J. xv
Searle, N. 17
Sharples, M. 16, 17, 36, 37
Siewert, R. xv
Stewart, J. 30
Stewart-Dore, J. 46, 49, 50
Straker, A. 33

Tolkien, J. R. R. 44

Walsh, W. xiii
Wilkinson, A. 59, 64
Wright, M. 21

PROGRAM INDEX

ADDVERSE 32, 44
CLASS READERS 11, 52
CLASS WRITER 11
DATAVIEW 89
EDFAX 48
FACTFILE 82
GLOT 45
INFOFILE 89, 91
KINGDOM 68
MALLORY 143–52
MARY ROSE 126, 159
NEWSDESK 70
POEM 36
QUEST 43, 77, 78, 85, 91, 159

SAQQARA 68
SEEK 30, 49
SLYFOX 73
SPACEX 124
STORYMAKER 31, 48, 71, 72
THE HOBBIT 44, 51, 52
TRAY 49, 52–5, 72, 128, 135–43, 159
TURNKEY 121
VIEWDATA 78, 123
WORDPLAY 33
WORDWISE 101
WRITE xv, 25